Pierre Favre SJ, the First Jesuit Companion

# By Way of the Heart

Brendan Comerford SJ

Published by Messenger Publications, 2025





ISBN 978-1-7881-2737-0

Designed by Brendan McCarthy
Typeset in Adobe Caslon Pro
Printed by Hussar Books

Milltown Park,
Dublin, D06W9Y7
Ireland
www.messenger.ie

*I would like to dedicate this book to my good friend, mentor and brother Jesuit Brian O'Leary SJ. Brian has been a source of constant encouragement and guidance to me in my reading in the history of Christian spirituality.*

*It was Brian's idea that I might attempt this book on St Pierre Favre. Brian is a world-renowned scholar in Ignatian spirituality and, especially, on the work of Favre. I am only too conscious that any errors or faults in this short book are to be attributed totally to myself!*

# Contents

# Prologue

On 13 March 2013, the Argentinian Jesuit Cardinal Jorge Mario Bergoglio was elected pope, taking the name 'Francis'; thereby evoking the memory and mission of that most famous and popular of saints, Francis of Assisi. Pope Francis was the first Jesuit in papal history to be elected to this highest office in the Roman Catholic Church. No member of a religious order had been chosen as pope since the time of Pope Gregory XVI (1831–1846). Gregory was a Camaldolese monk.[1]

On 14 June 2013, Antonio Spadaro SJ, editor-in-chief of the Jesuit journal *La Civilità Cattolica*, had an extensive interview with this then newly elected pope.[2] In the course of this interview, Pope Francis stressed three key words that would describe his future mission as pope: 'dialogue', 'discernment' and 'frontiers'. These three words/approaches to mission will be seen in this book as being key to the life and ministry of Pierre Favre.

In the course of the interview with Pope Francis, Spadaro asked him who his favourite Jesuit was among the early companions of St Ignatius Loyola (1491–1556). Without a moment's hesitation, Pope Francis answered, 'Pierre Favre.' When asked why, Francis replied:

> His [Favre's] dialogue with all, even the most remote and even with his opponents; his simple piety, a certain naiveté perhaps, his being available straightaway, his careful interior discernment, the fact that he was a man capable of great and strong decisions but also capable of being so gentle and loving.

It is hoped that in reading this book, you, the reader, will find many echoes of these qualities in the life and mission of Pierre Favre.

On 17 December 2013, Pope Francis telephoned the then superior general of the Society of Jesus, Adolfo Nicolás, to tell the superior general that he 'had just signed the document'.

Nicolás knew immediately what document the pope was referring to – it was the document authorising the canonisation of Pierre Favre. The pope's edict of canonisation was termed 'an equipollent canonisation', 'equipollent' meaning 'of equal value'. Equal value to what you might well ask – equal to a formal canonisation ceremony without all the ritual that goes with it. The pope's document was sufficient. The late Pope Emeritus Benedict XVI canonised the twelfth-century German mystic Hildegard of Bingen (1098–1179) in exactly the same way. An equipollent canonisation can be performed for a figure, deemed to be of particular relevance in the Church, for whom there has been a popular, liturgical devotion over the years.[3]

Devotion to Pierre Favre extended back many centuries. Favre died on 1 August 1546 and, shortly afterwards, Ignatius Loyola was invoking Favre's intercession. His close friend and former roommate while at the University of Paris, the famous Jesuit missionary in the East, Francis Xavier, included Favre's name in his personal litany of the saints: *Sancte Petre Faber, ora pro nobis*. At the time of Favre's death, in some places, Masses of thanksgiving for his life and ministry were celebrated instead of Masses for the dead. Favre's letters and personal belongings were treated as relics.[4]

In 1607, St Francis de Sales, bishop of Geneva, consecrated an altar in Favre's honour in Villaret, his birthplace, in Savoy, France. In 1612, Francis, while returning a book which a Jesuit, Nicolas Polliens, had loaned him 'of the holy life … of our blessed Pierre Favre', wrote:

> I would have wished to have a copy of this story [*Memoriale*] of a saint to whom, for many reasons, I have

> a devotion ... However, I would like to believe that, in good time, the Society of Jesus would resolve not to give less honour to this first companion of its founder than that it has given to others.[5]

The process for the beatification of Pierre Favre began in 1626. This process was undertaken by Bishop Jean-François de Sales, brother of St Francis de Sales and his eventual successor as bishop of Geneva. Around the same time, Favre's beatification was also requested by eighty-seven priests who had gathered for a retreat in the seminary in Annecy. They wrote:

> We, the priests of the Diocese of Annecy, marvel that this man of God, first companion of St Ignatius of Loyola, first priest and preacher of the divine Word, this cornerstone of the Society of Jesus, this tireless worker in the Lord's vineyard ... has not been included and venerated among the saints ...[6]

Outside the circle of the Society of Jesus and the territory of Savoy, Pierre Favre was little known or venerated. Promoters of his canonisation would have a long wait. Favre was eventually beatified on 5 September 1872 by Pope Pius IX. 141 years later, on 17 December 2013, Favre was finally canonised. Pope Francis brought to a conclusion this long process on the road to sainthood, a process which began eighty years after Favre's death.

But, who was this Pierre Favre?

**Notes**

1. While revising this chapter in May 2025, I rejoice at the election of Pope Leo XIV, an Augustinian friar!
2. This interview was published in *La Civiltà Cattolica*, 21 September 2013. The interview was also conducted on behalf of the Jesuit magazine *America* and several other Jesuit journals around the world. For an English-language edition, see Antonio Spadaro, 'A Big Heart Open to God: An Interview with Pope Francis', *America*, www.americamagazine.org/faith/2013/09/30/big-heart-open-god-interview-pope-francis

3. Antonio Spadaro, *Pietro Favre: Servitore della Consolazionea* (Milan: La Civiltà Cattolica, 2013), p. 9.
4. Spadaro, *Pietro Favre*, pp. 9–10.
5. Francis de Sales, *Introduction to the Devout Life*, trans. and ed by John K. Ryan (New York: Image Books, 1972), part II, paragraph 16. Here Francis refers to Favre as 'blessed', p. 107.
6. Spadaro, *Pietro Favre*, p. 10.

# Part One:
# His Journeys

Journeys of Pierre Favre

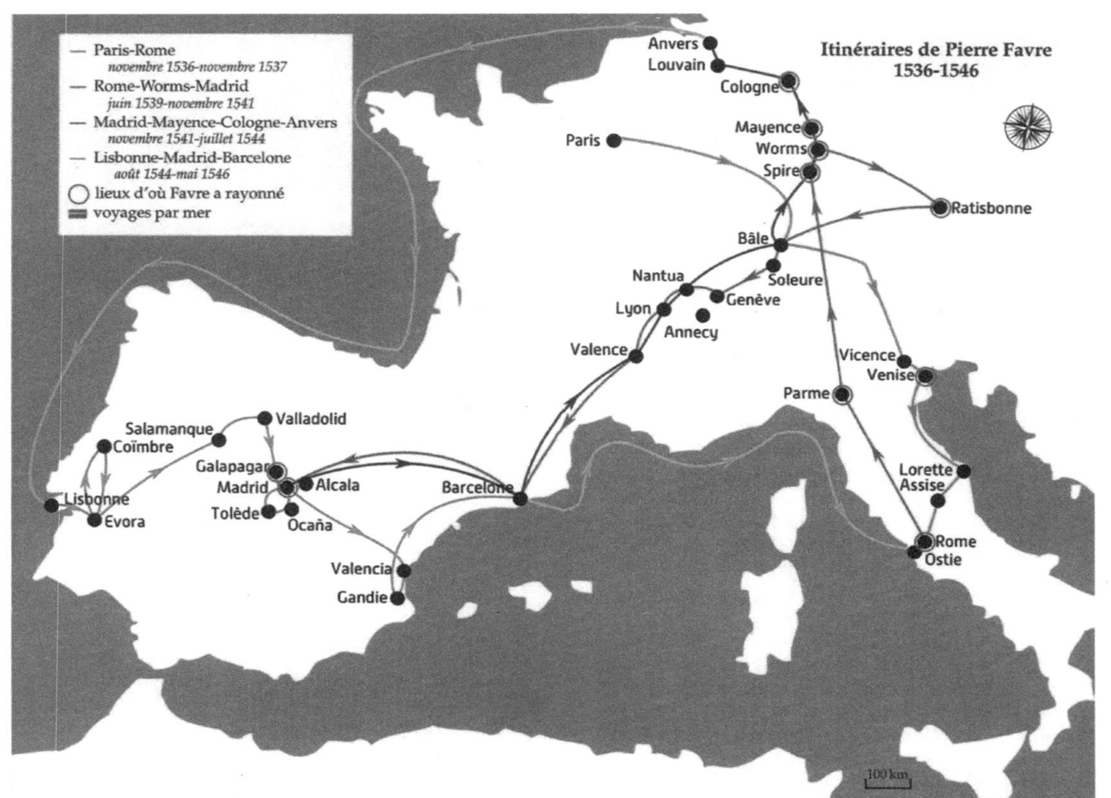

## Chapter 1

# The Early Years (1506–1525)

Pierre Favre was born on Easter Monday, 13 April 1506, in a village named Villaret in the alpine region of the Grand-Bornand in Savoy, south-eastern France. He was baptised on the same day in the parish church of St-Jean-de-Sixt by the local curé, Antoine Agniellet. Pierre's parents, Louis Favre and Marie Périssin,[1] were natives of the Grand-Bornand – a region of stupendous beauty.[2] Pierre had two younger brothers, petit-Louis and Jean. Pierre's family lived a pastoral existence near the River Borne in this mountain hamlet of Villaret.

What is this region of Savoy like? The Alps confront the Savoyards at every turn. In summer and winter these mountains impose a way of life on the shepherds of the region. In the sixteenth century, Catholicism marked the lives of the Savoyards: the example and inspiration of the saints influenced their lives; the shrines of the Virgin Mary dot the land to this day.[3] We will see, in later chapters, how veneration of local saints figures very strongly in Pierre's personal spirituality.

Savoy was a region of strong traditional piety. The Confraternity of the Holy Spirit was established in nearly all parishes. This confraternity encouraged the practice of works of charity among the local inhabitants – from each person the confraternity collected offerings of crops, firewood, fleeces, meat and other necessities of life for distribution among the needy, the sick, widows, orphans and the aged.[4]

In his spiritual journal, the *Memoriale*, Pierre describes his parents as 'good and very pious Catholic parents'[5] who brought him up 'in the fear of the Lord'. 'Fear of the Lord' was to play a considerable part in Pierre's spiritual life, even from an early age. He recalls how 'while yet still young, I began to be conscious of myself'.[6] Pierre means by this that he was fearful of transgressing the law of God. At an early age, he began to take stock of his behaviour, to examine his conscience. This will be the beginning of a lifelong habit of introspection.[7]

The Favre family were farmers and shepherds, the only way to survive in those alpine regions. During the winters, when deep snow covered the hamlets and villages, little movement was possible.[8] Every May, when the snow melted in the Grand-Bornand and the adjoining valleys of Savoy, the farm animals were moved up to the alpine pastures.

On Sundays and feast days, Pierre went to Mass in the parish church of St-Jean-de-Sixt, where he heard the priest's sermons and religious instruction. Contemporary accounts credit him with a quick and retentive memory, capable of repeating word for word what the priest had said. This Pierre would do standing on a rock, his congregation being a group of local children! Adults who stopped to listen paid 'dues' in the shape of berries, nuts and apples. People of the village referred to the young Pierre as *petit prédicateur* and *petit docteur*, the 'little preacher' or 'little doctor'.

Some weeks before his seventh birthday in 1513, Pierre was sent as a shepherd of sheep to the *alpage* (mountain pasture) for the first time. This was a rough and responsible outdoor life in the company of the other shepherds of the area. Very soon Pierre began to realise that he had neither taste nor aptitude for this life his parents had planned for him. He wanted to go to school.

Before he was even ten years old, Pierre had an intense desire to study:

> I was a shepherd and my parents intended me for the world. Each night in bed I wept, so great was my longing to be educated ... In spite of themselves, my parents agreed to send me to school. Then, seeing my progress,

> they allowed me to continue studying … Besides, God made me very inept and quite useless for anything else.[9]

Here, already, we see an example of Pierre's self-deprecating humour.

## Early schooling

At first, Pierre went to elementary school at Thônes, a town situated on the River Fier, about six miles from Villaret. Here he was taught reading, writing and grammar, probably by one Jacques Crozet, who had opened a school in Thônes.[10] In only seven months, Pierre had out-distanced all the other little scholars.

A year later, in 1517, Pierre's parents sent him to La Roche-sur-Furon, about twelve miles northwest of Villaret, on the road between Annecy and Bonneville. Hundreds of pupils flocked to La Roche-sur-Furon that autumn. News had percolated through the valleys that the famous Swiss teacher Pierre Veillard had come there to teach.[11]

Veillard was a holy priest who made a deep impression on Pierre. He revered Veillard as a saint, prayed to Veillard when he died and made a point of visiting his grave when passing through Savoy in later years. Veillard was very much influenced by the Brethren of the Common Life,[12] especially in their devotion to the humanity of Christ. Even more than Veillard, the Carthusian monks of the nearby monastery of Le Reposoir brought Pierre within the spiritual influence of Gerard Groote,[13] Ludolf of Saxony[14] and Jan van Ruysbroeck.[15]

In his *Memoriale*, Favre writes:

> When I was about twelve years of age, I had certain impulses from the Holy Spirit to offer myself for the service of God our Lord, and one day, during the holiday time, I went into a field where from time to time I helped to guard the flocks, and there, full of joy and with a great

> desire for purity, I vowed perpetual chastity to God our Lord.[16]

Nowadays we would be more than wary of this type of private vow made at such a tender age. Later we will see that the subject of chastity crops up quite frequently in the *Memoriale*. One wonders why?

Besides the usual school subjects, Pierre Veillard also taught the classics of Greek and Latin literature 'in such a way as to make them seem like the Gospels'.[17] In addition to the classics, Veillard taught extracts from the early Fathers of the Church and from the *Sentences* of Peter Lombard – this was the classic theology textbook of the time.[18] Favre displayed an unusual flair for Greek. He remained at the school in La Roche until aged nineteen. One of Favre's fellow students, but in a higher class, was one Claude Jay.[19] Jay was three years older than Favre. The two boys became close friends. Jay was to remain on in Savoy for some years, eventually succeeding Veillard as principal of the La Roche school. Jay and Favre were to meet again in unforeseen circumstances.

Pierre's paternal uncle was Dom Mamert Favre, since 1508 prior of the Carthusian monastery of Le Reposoir, some ten miles from Villaret. Dom Mamert was prior until 1522. As a boy, it is likely that Favre would have visited Le Reposoir and seen the white-robed, silent monks. He would have been shown and handled the printed books in the monastery library. Tradition tells us that Dom Mamert was very interested in his young nephew and gave Favre's parents constant guidance and support. His maternal cousin, Dom Claude Périssan, became prior in 1522. In the monastic annals of Le Reposoir, Dom Claude is referred to as 'a man of singular piety, extraordinary skill, gifted by nature and grace for the office of governing'.[20] He directed Favre to Paris for his further studies and put him in touch with the Carthusians at Vauvert, a monastery only a short distance from the Collège of Sainte Barbe where Favre was to study. Some famous Carthusians were teachers in Sainte Barbe.[21] This college was founded in 1460 in what is now the locale of the Luxembourg Palace and Gardens in Paris.

In the autumn of 1517, news of epoch-making events in Germany was brought to La Roche by travellers riding south from Geneva. At Halloween, an Augustinian friar, Martin Luther, had nailed his ninety-five theses to the doors of the college chapel in Wittenberg, Germany.[22] Some weeks later, a Swiss priest, Ulrich Zwingli,[23] told his congregation that many religious practices were useless and that he had buried relics to prevent people from venerating them! The Reformation had begun.

Notes

1. In the canonical process of beatification of Favre, begun in 1626, Peter Critan, parish priest of Thônes, testified that Pierre's parents were good Catholics, like all the family, and never suspected of heresy. Others affirmed that they frequented the sacraments and were never excommunicated! See Spadaro, *Pietro Favre*, p. 16.
2. Le Grand-Bornand is the name of a valley through which the River Bornand flows. It is also the name of a parish. See William V. Bangert, *To the Other Towns: A Life of Peter Favre* (San Francisco: Ignatius Press, 2002), p. 16.
3. See *The Spiritual Writings of Pierre Favre*, ed by Edmond C. Murphy and John W. Padberg (St Louis, MO: Institute of Jesuit Sources, 1996), p. 8.
4. *Spiritual Writings of Pierre Favre*, p. 8.
5. Pierre Favre, *Memoriale*, 1. Quotations from the *Memoriale* are taken from *Spiritual Writings of Pierre Favre*.
6. *Memoriale*, 2.
7. See *Spiritual Writings of Pierre Favre*, p. 61.
8. Brian O'Leary, 'The Discernment of Spirits in the *Memoriale* of Blessed Peter Favre', *The Way Supplement*, 35 (1979), p. 9.
9. *Memoriale*, 3.
10. Spadaro, *Pietro Favre*, p. 19.
11. In 1517 Viellard published a volume entitled *Modus Componendi Epistolas* (*Manner of Composing Letters*), cf. Bangert, *To the Other Towns*, p. 21.
12. The Brethren of the Common Life was an association founded in the fourteenth century to foster a higher level of Christian life and devotion. The original founder was Gerard Groote, a canon of Utrecht. Groote's followers founded schools in Germany and the Netherlands. They adopted a rule as Augustinian canons.
13. Gerard Groote (1340–1384) founded the Brethren of the Common Life.
14. Ludolf of Saxony (d. 1338) was a Carthusian monk. His most famous work was the *Vita Christi*, a book of meditations on the life of Christ. Ignatius of Loyola read this work during his recuperation after the battle of Pamplona.
15. Jan van Ruysbroeck (1293–1381) was prominent in the religious movement later known as the *Devotio Moderna* with which were also associated the Brethren of the Common Life and the Canons Regular of Windesheim and such an eminent writer as Thomas à Kempis.
16. *Memoriale*, 4.
17. *Memoriale*, 3.
18. Peter Lombard (c. 1100–1160), the 'Master of the Sentences', was born in Lombardy, Italy; he went to Reims and then c. 1134 to Paris where he taught at the Cathedral School. In 1159, shortly before his death, he was appointed bishop of Paris. The *Sentences* was the standard textbook of Catholic theology during the Middle Ages.

19. Claude Jay (c. 1500–1552) was born in Upper Savoy. Like Favre, he too studied at La Roche. Ordained a priest in 1523 in Geneva, he went to Paris in 1534 to improve his theology. Favre will give the Spiritual Exercises to Jay in Paris. Jay joined the early companions of St Ignatius Loyola. He will later lecture in theology in Germany and will be present at the Council of Trent. He was almost appointed bishop of Trieste. Jay died in Vienna in 1552.
20. In Bangert, *To the Other Towns*, p. 25.
21. The Carthusians, Pierre de Cornet and François Le Picart were especially influential in Paris academic circles of the time. See Spadaro, *Pietro Favre*, p. 19.
22. In 1517, Dominican Johann Tetzel (c. 1465–1519) was preaching that Pope Leo X would grant indulgences to those who would contribute to the renovation of St Peter's Basilica. In response, Luther drew up his famous ninety-five theses, condemning the preaching of Tetzel, as well as other teachings of the Roman Catholic Church. Within a fortnight, the ninety-five theses had spread throughout Germany and further beyond, where they were welcomed by those desiring the reform of the Church.
23. Ulrich Zwingli (1484–1531) was ordained priest in 1506. Zwingli became a Swiss reformer. In his sermons, he attacked the doctrine of purgatory. He also attacked the invocation of the saints and monasticism. He preached the liberation of believers from the control of the papacy and of bishops. The sacrifice of the Mass, times and seasons of fasting and clerical celibacy were rejected. He taught a purely symbolic interpretation of the Eucharist.

Chapter 2

# Paris (1525–1536)

At the age of nineteen, Pierre left his own countryside of Savoy and walked the 350 miles to Paris. His studies in Paris were to last from 1525–1536. On arrival in Paris, he was older by four or five years than the average first-year students. He was also much more advanced than them in Latin and Greek.

Paris was then a city of some 300,000 inhabitants. The University of Paris functioned through almost fifty separate colleges. These colleges served as residences for intern students and professors. The university concentrated on theology, philosophy and letters; but by far the most numerous among the faculties was that of Arts, dedicated mostly to the study of the Greek philosopher Aristotle.

Pierre's college was to be Sainte Barbe. This was a new and prosperous college (founded in 1460), which had a high academic reputation. It had amenities unknown to other colleges, which it owed to the generous patronage of the Portuguese kings, especially King John III. It was a humanist stronghold holding the doctrine of letters for letters' sake.[1] The majority of the students were Portuguese. There were about 220 students, in all, at Sainte Barbe. The principal or rector of the college was Diogo de Gouveia (1520–1529), a Portuguese nobleman, highly regarded in academic and in royal circles (the court of King John III of Portugal).

The College of Sainte Barbe, encouraged by its rector, had gone over to humanism and was devoting itself to the Greek and Latin classics. It boasted some distinguished professors, many of whom were humanists and followers of Desiderius Erasmus.[2] Erasmus advocated the reform of religion by a return to the sources, above all the New Testament in its original Greek and, secondly, the Greek and Latin Fathers of the Church. It is likely that Favre read some of Erasmus's works and listened to his ideas for the reform of the Church.

Favre found himself sharing a room in Sainte Barbe with a young regent,[3] Juan de La Peña,[4] who had just graduated the previous summer. Favre was to live with La Peña, his tutor, for eleven years; so La Peña must have exerted an influence on him, in matters philosophical and theological. Another student who shared rooms with Favre and La Peña was Francis Xavier, from Navarre, Spain. Although Favre and Xavier quickly became friends, they could not have been more different. Favre, a shepherd from Savoy, pious, reserved, sensitive and studious; his affable manner and tranquil exterior masking an inner turmoil that, at times, drove him almost to despair. Xavier, a nobleman from Navarre, was ambitious and inclined to haughtiness, claiming as his ancestors nobles and persons of great distinction and pre-eminence in the realm of Navarre. Xavier was also a promising athlete and one of the finest vaulters on the Ile da la Cité. He was less enthusiastic about study than Favre. Xavier spent most of his time at the students' playing fields, the Pré-aux-Clercs.[5]

Favre and Xavier, coming from remote, wholly Catholic areas of the alpine and Pyrenean foothills, must have been confused during their first term in Sainte Barbe, hearing about the Lutheran reformers. In Paris, Lutherans began, at this time, an open campaign against Catholicism. Posters depicting the pope as anti-Christ were affixed to church walls and public buildings. Speakers in the street attacked fundamental doctrines of the Roman Catholic Church. On 2 March 1521, the faculty of theology at the Sorbonne condemned a great number of Lutheran works – they were considered to be heretical.

## Nominalism

By the time Favre had arrived in Paris, nominalism, a system of philosophy elaborated initially by the Franciscan William of Ockham,[6] had superseded almost all other kinds of philosophy in the universities of Europe. Nominalism gave rise to a broad current of philosophy and theology called the *via moderna* (new way). It challenged traditional scholastic philosophy and theology, the *via antiqua*.[7]

The representatives of the *via antiqua*, followers of Thomas Aquinas,[8] were realists. They held that universal concepts are the expression of reality. In contrast, for the followers of the *via moderna,* what is real is the individual. Nominalism stressed the importance of the individual as opposed to the universal, the abstract, and thus emphasised the value of experience. Nominalism undermined belief in the possibility of objective knowledge. For the nominalist, universals do not exist in reality, rather they are posited by the mind primarily through language.[9]

We will see that for Favre and the early Jesuits experience was of the greatest importance in the spiritual life. They looked on experience as 'given' them by God: it revealed God's will.[10] The will of God makes itself known to the heart and gives greater certainty than one could gain from a mere intellectual understanding of the faith. In experience, they read 'signs' of God's plan for them.

The University of Paris itself was the great centre of nominalist thought as interpreted by Gabriel Biel, who was regarded as the leading nominalist theologian of the fifteenth century.[11] Biel wrote a commentary on the *Sentences* of Peter Lombard. It was Biel's teaching, as presented by various professors of theology in Paris, including Favre's tutor, Juan de La Peña, that helped form the early Jesuits.

Gabriel Biel's *Commentary on the Sentences of Peter Lombard* became the most popular compendium of theology in the universities of Europe. It played a major part in the theological formation of Favre. He had been taught a will-based theology that stressed personal relationships with God, and that led him to seek in interior experience for the sign that he was accepted by God.

During Favre's time in Paris the ideas of traditional Scholasticism (especially at the Collège de Sorbonne), nominalism, humanism and Protestantism all crossed and recrossed in the narrow streets of the Latin Quarter. The theologians at the Sorbonne (mostly Scholastics) thundered that 'the new teaching [humanism] was scandalous, heretical and tainted with Lutheranism'.[12]

We know the names of some of Favre's professors in Paris – all of them adherents to nominalism, to a greater or lesser extent. Favre gives these names in a letter written to the rector of Sainte-Barbe, Diogo de Gouveia.[13]

## A student's day at Sainte Barbe

Students, at Sainte Barbe, rose at 4am. First class was at 5am, followed by Mass at 6am. They were then given some dry bread and a glass of watered-down wine. The second class lasted from 8am–10am, followed by time for questions, discussions and reviews for an hour. At 11am, everyone went to the refectory. During the meal a student read from Sacred Scripture or the Lives of the Saints. The third class lasted from 3pm to 5pm; next came discussion and reviews (again!), followed by supper at 6pm. After that, there was a review in class of the whole day! Following a visit to the Blessed Sacrament, the bell gave the signal for all to retire. Bed was at 8pm or 9pm, depending on the season.

On Saturdays, the morning was devoted to reviewing the week's lessons and the afternoon to a disputation in the great hall. Six days a year, the schedules were shortened to permit the students to go to confession to the Dominicans of the nearby priory. This took place at the beginning of Lent, at Easter, at Pentecost, on the Assumption, on All Saints and at Christmas.

Latin was the usual language of instruction. Latin was also spoken during day-to-day activities because, in a place where so many students came from different parts of Europe, Latin was the easiest way of making oneself understood. The university required that all students would know how to speak Latin correctly and offered one year of Latin studies to the new students. Both Xavier and Favre followed this proffered course – they felt that they needed some time to polish their Latin before they undertook more demanding studies.

## Studies in philosophy

Before Favre had been a year in Sainte Barbe, his proficiency in Greek had been noted. This entitled him to a bourse (scholarship) reserved for students other than Portuguese. Even the regents, including Favre's teacher Juan de La Peña, when in doubt as to how a certain passage in Aristotle should be rendered referred the matter to Favre!

In October 1526, after this year of preparatory studies, Favre and Xavier began their three and a half years' philosophy course under the direction of Juan de La Peña. These initial studies would have been the *trivium*, the traditional foundation of every good liberal arts education: grammar, dialectic and rhetoric. This involved intensive study of Plato, Aristotle and Boethius, as well as logic and the art of argument. Students would be taught how to present and defend their ideas with clarity, while, at the same time, exposing the weakness of their opponent's arguments. Later would come the *quadrivium* of arithmetic, astronomy, geometry and music. Favre would also have read Cicero, Augustine, Peter Lombard, Peter Abelard and Thomas Aquinas.

Favre became a Bachelor of Arts on 10 January 1529 at the age of twenty-three. This degree entitled the student to teach the lower classes of the colleges, thus becoming a regent. In order to take the Licentiate in Arts degree, it was necessary to study Aristotle's *Ethics, Physics* and *Metaphysics*, as well as some elements of astronomy and mathematics. At Sainte Barbe, where the environment was very Portuguese, particular importance was attached to geography and navigational science – this, after all, was the age of the discovery of new lands.

On 3 February 1530, the exams for the Licentiate began at the Collège de Sainte Geneviève in the presence of Chancellor Jacques Aimery. There were four examiners, one from each nation of the university (France, Italy, Spain, Portugal). Both Favre and Xavier acquitted themselves well. On 15 March, they had to swear on the Gospel that they would be faithful to their duties as teachers. They pronounced a solemn formula that authorised them to teach 'at Paris and anywhere else in the world'.

The Licentiate examination involved great expense for, besides the prescribed fees, the graduates had to put on a banquet for their teachers and fellow students. In the history of the university, in the catalogue of abuses, the payments made or extorted on the occasion of graduation came up often. It was sometimes the ruination of the poorer students![14]

After Easter 1530, Favre and Xavier were awarded the Licentiate in Arts, under Juan de La Peña. Favre postponed any banquet. Now the only thing that stood in his way of receiving the Master's degree was the financial wherewithal! No strict examination was required for this degree but endless expense was involved. Whereas Favre's purse could not take the financial strain, Xavier had sufficient funds, and so he became 'Master Francis' in March 1530. Favre postponed taking the Master's degree until the spring of 1536 – purely for financial reasons.

Favre now began his studies in theology, but he was unable to make up his mind about his future. This indecision, a form of diffidence and mistrust of self, would reveal itself in later years as exaggerated dependence on orders from superiors when faced, on occasion, with important decisions.

## Ignatius of Loyola arrives in Paris

Let's go back a year to 1529. The university year began on 1 October, St Remi's Day. On that date, a Basque nobleman, Ignatius Loyola, moved into lodgings with Favre and Xavier. Ignatius was thirty-seven and had spent the previous eighteen months studying

Latin at the Collège de Montaigu. This college had roughly 120 students under the direction of the Carthusian prior of the monastery of Vauvert. Ignatius was fifteen years older than Favre and Xavier. Favre began to coach Ignatius in Latin and in Aristotle. According to a second-generation Jesuit, Pedro de Ribadeneira,[15] when Ignatius began his philosophical studies, there was an agreement between himself and Favre that they would not speak about spiritual matters in their study time; otherwise Ignatius would get so carried away by a surge of divine love that he would forget everything else, get swept away in long discourses and use up the time.[16]

To his dying day, Favre never ceased to thank God for so arranging things that he should teach Ignatius about Aristotle while Ignatius taught him about God:

> He [Ignatius] became my spiritual teacher and gave me rules for ascertaining the will of God ... In the end, we became one in desire and will and one in a firm resolve to take up that life we live today – we the future members of this Society of which I am unworthy.
>
> May it please the divine clemency to give me the grace of clearly remembering and pondering the benefits which the Lord conferred on me through that man. Firstly, he gave me an understanding of my conscience and of the temptations and scruples I had for so long without either understanding them or seeing the way by which I would be able to get peace.
>
> The scruples were over the fear that over a long period of time I had not properly confessed my sins, which gave me so much anxiety ... The temptations that I experienced at that time were over evil and foul carnal images suggested by the spirit of fornication.
>
> Iñigo advised me to make a general confession to Dr Castro[17] and to go to confession and communion once a week for the future. To help me in this, he gave me the daily Examination of Conscience, unwilling to put me

> through other exercises for the time being, though our Lord was giving me a great longing for them.
>
> In that way we passed about four years together … My soul was passing through many fires of temptation and waters of vain-glory … for which I sought a remedy during a long and anguished time … With regard to gluttony also I had many struggles, and I was unable to find peace until the time of the Exercises. When in Paris, sometimes I resented certain orders of Ignatius and I used to say to him that in France people would not stand for things that he seemed to think fitting.
>
> Our Lord instructed me in so many ways, giving me remedies against so many bouts of depression … He would grant me grace to ask, to seek, and to knock for that grace … That remedy included countless graces to recognise and to experience the different spirits with which I was getting more acquainted from day to day, for the Lord had left in me those goads [*espuelas*], which never let me remain lukewarm.[18]

We see from the above that Ignatius taught Favre the proper discernment of the various spirits (good and evil) that might assail him. Favre is totally honest with himself here – he remembers the attacks of the bad spirit, causing scrupulosity and temptations against chastity. Remember this is the young man who made a personal vow of chastity at the age of twelve. How unwise that was! Favre also acknowledges how the bad spirits of gluttony and vainglory would assail him. These experiences of the attack of bad spirits caused Favre to experience bouts of depression – this would be a recurring psychological experience throughout his life. Favre's confession of human weakness and mental fragility makes him a most attractive saint. Favre is one of us! It's even amusing to know that there were some small moments of tension between Ignatius and Favre, with the latter taking exception, at least once, to the manner in which Ignatius addressed him.

Pedro de Ribadeneira tells us that Ignatius did not suddenly overwhelm Favre with his spiritual power; rather, he 'proceeded little by little' with Favre. As we will see, it will be a whole four years before Ignatius guides Favre through the entire Spiritual Exercises (a retreat of thirty days).[19]

In March 1530, having finished the necessary requirements for the Master of Arts degree (apart from the cash and the banquet!). Favre continued to live at Saint Barbe and began his study of theology in various colleges. Xavier went to teach Aristotle at Collège de Dormans-Beauvais. He lived there, very close to Sainte Barbe.

Xavier did not yield to Ignatius's spiritual direction as readily as Favre. 'In spiritual matters he was not much taken by him,' wrote the Jesuit Juan de Polanco, secretary to Ignatius Loyola, when, later, Ignatius was superior general of the Society of Jesus.[20]

Ignatius had to pave the way to winning Xavier's friendship by inducing students to attend Xavier's classes. Five years later, Xavier would write to his brother, Juan, that he would never be able to repay his debt to Ignatius for having helped him with money and friends and for having saved him from ill-advised company.

Around October of 1532, Ignatius had won the friendship of a young Portuguese student at Sainte Barbe, Simão Rodrigues.[21] Rodrigues had been in Paris since 1527. We will now begin to see the number of early companions gradually increasing.

Near the Latin Quarter of Paris, where the early companions lived, was the urban Carthusian Charterhouse of Vauvert, whose monks were engaged in both the academic and spiritual life. The companions were accustomed to go to this monastery for confession, Mass and spiritual conversation on Sundays.

### Favre returns to Savoy

In early June 1533, Favre returned to Savoy to visit his family and relations. In the years since his departure from home in 1525, Favre's mother had died. He remained in Savoy for some seven months. While there, he requested the local diocesan office give him the documents authorising him to be ordained priest. Favre encountered his old school friend at La Roche, Claude Jay, now a priest since 1528. He persuaded Jay to come to Paris to complete his theological studies. Jay did so in 1534 and enrolled at the Collège Sainte Barbe. One of Jay's classmates there was a certain Paschase Broët,[22] a priest of the Diocese of Picardy. Broët had been ordained in Amiens in 1524. After working for ten years, he came to Paris to complete his studies and enrolled at the Collège de Calvi. Jay and Broët were later to take Favre as their spiritual director during these Paris years. Bröet, too, would join the first companions. In addition, a certain Jean Codure left the mountains of Provence in southern France and came to Paris to study for the priesthood. In 1534, he enrolled for the Collège de Lisieux, which was near the Collège Sainte Barbe. Codure too would be numbered among the early companions.

## Spiritual Exercises

In January 1534, Favre returned to Paris. On his arrival, he discovered that Ignatius had three more companions to introduce to him, all Spaniards: Diego Laínez, Alfonso Salmerón and Nicolás Bobadilla.[23]

This winter of 1534 was particularly harsh. The River Seine was completely frozen over – so much so that carriages could cross over it. It was at this very time that Favre did the Spiritual Exercises under the direction of Ignatius. He was the first of the early companions of Ignatius to do so.

During the retreat, Favre stayed in a house on the Faubourg Saint-Jacques. Ignatius would come to visit him every other day to give instructions and spiritual advice. He paid attention to seeing whether Favre's lips were sticking together in order to know if Favre was eating.[24] It seems that Favre had not eaten or hardly drank for the first six days of the retreat! He only drank a cup of wine after receiving Holy Communion. He lit no fire and slept on the timber given him for a fire. He made his meditations in the courtyard in the snow. All this seemed too excessive to Ignatius. He went away to reflect on Favre's penitential exercises, returned and ordered Favre to moderate his fervour, to light a fire and to be sure to eat.

During this retreat, Favre endured times of sadness, anxiety, scruples, hesitation and fear – all part of his nature. Yet the experience of doing the Spiritual Exercises would be central in Favre's future spiritual life, especially in relation to the discernment of the various spirits. Ignatius would give the Spiritual Exercises to Diego Laínez and Alfonso Salmerón during the spring of the same year, to Nicolás Bobadilla and Simão Rodrigues shortly afterwards and, finally, to Francis Xavier the following September.

Having experienced the Spiritual Exercises himself, Favre would later give the Exercises to Claude Jay, Paschase Broët and Jean Codure. Giving the Spiritual Exercises was a ministry in which Favre was to excel. He was said by Ignatius to be the most skilled among the early companions in directing the Exercises.[25]

## Ordination

Before his priestly ordination, Favre tells us:

> Before that – I mean before having settled upon the course of my life through the help given me by God through Iñigo – I was always very unsure of myself and blown about by many winds: sometimes wishing to be married, sometimes to be a doctor, sometimes a lawyer, ... sometimes a professor of theology, sometimes a cleric ... at times wishing to be a monk. I was borne about previously by these winds, according as the greater of the lesser heavenly body was dominant that is, according as one or other attraction reigned. Delivering me ... from these attractions by the consolation of his Spirit, our Lord led me to a firm decision to become a priest completely dedicated to his service.[26]

Some commentators see these attitudes, fleeting ideas, momentary attractions as being characteristic of immaturity and adolescence and that Favre's inner turmoil and the suffering it caused him were psychological in origin.[27] Finally, at any rate, Favre opted for priesthood.

On 28 February 1534, very shortly after he had finished the Spiritual Exercises, Favre was ordained a sub-deacon in the Gothic chapel of the episcopal palace, near Notre Dame, by Millo d'Illiers, bishop of Luçon. This was in the absence of the bishop of Paris, Jean du Bellay, then in Rome about the business of the divorce of King Henry VIII from Queen Catherine of Aragon. On 4 April, Favre was ordained a deacon in the same chapel by the Augustinian Laurent Alamandis, bishop of Grenoble. Du Bellay was back in Paris by the end of May and, on 30 May 1534, the eve of Trinity Sunday, he ordained Favre priest. Favre waited almost two months before offering his first Mass on 22 July 1534. He remembers: 'I said my First Mass on the feast of the Blessed Mary Magdalene, my advocate and advocate of all other sinners, men and women.'[28]

Perhaps Favre delayed saying his first Mass for these two months because the documents giving proof of his title (to be a priest) had not yet arrived from his native Diocese of Annecy. We might bear in mind here too that Ignatius delayed saying his first Mass for one-and-a-half years after his ordination! As for his own call to priestly ministry, Favre would later write:

> I shall never, of my own merits, be equal to the demands of the priesthood or be worthy of God's choice. But the very recognition of this obliges me to do my utmost, physically and spiritually, to respond to his call.[29]

We shall see, later, just how generously Favre devoted all his energies, mental, physical and spiritual, to his ministry as a priest.

## Vows at Montmartre

On the morning of 14 August 1534, the feast of the Assumption of the Blessed Virgin, Favre, Ignatius Loyola, Xavier and four other companions[30] met in the crypt of the Chapel of Saint-Denis on Montmartre, just north of Paris, and pronounced vows of chastity, of evangelical poverty (as soon as their studies at the university were completed) and also a vow to make a pilgrimage to the Holy Land, if transport could be found within a year of their leaving Paris. Favre was the first and only priest among them. He celebrated the Mass and held up the consecrated host, just before Holy Communion, as the companions pronounced their vows. Simão gave an account of this ceremony many years later:

> No outsider was present, just the Fathers [They were not yet priests]. Fr Favre celebrated Mass and before he gave communion to his companions, he turned to them and held the sacred host in his hands. They were kneeling on the floor with their minds fixed on God, and each in his turn pronounced the vows in a clear voice audible to all. Then they all received Holy Communion together. Turning to the altar, Father [Favre], in the same way, before consuming the life-giving bread, pronounced his vows so distinctly and clearly that he was heard by everyone.[31]

The companions were to repeat this practice of pronouncing these same vows on 15 August 1535 and 1536.

## L'Affaire des Placards

On the night of 17 October 1534, placards speaking against the Roman Catholic Mass were posted on the walls of Paris, Orleáns, Tours and Blois and even on King Francis I's private chambers in the Château d'Amboise. This episode, which came to be known as L'Affaire des Placards, was inspired by one Antoine Marcourt, a pastor in Neuchâtel, who professed some of the radical ideas of Ulrich Zwingli. Marcourt questioned the real presence of Christ in the Eucharist. King Francis reacted promptly to such 'heresies'. A police investigation was launched and some 200 people were jailed. A few hundred metres from Sainte Barbe, execution fires were lit on the Place Maubert. At the end of November, a printer of 'heretical books', Antoine Augereau, was burned to death. From January to May of 1535, there would be up to twenty-five deaths by burning. At the same time, there were numerous burnings of Lutheran books in front of Notre Dame Cathedral. Favre must have been a witness to all of this religious tension and tragedy.[32]

It was compulsory for the student body to be present at the execution of a 'heretic'. Time and again, during the winter of 1534–35, classes were suspended while the students were marched out to witness the burning and torturing of heretics. These acts of violence ended up shocking even the Catholics themselves. Pope Paul III requested that these unhealthy passions be restrained.

Favre spent eleven years at Sainte Barbe, his intellectual formation being more literary and philosophical than theological. He attended lectures in theology where they were offered: at the convent of the Dominicans and the Franciscans, both in Rue Saint-Jacques, at the Sorbonne, and at the Collège de Navarre. Favre became a competent pastoral theologian, nothing more; he was intelligent but not an intellectual. He was never to receive his doctorate. In his mind, theological speculation would take second place to an exclusive concern with bringing people back to God.

## Ignatius leaves for Spain

At the beginning of April 1535, Ignatius left Paris for Spain. He had been advised because of his poor health to take his native air. He appointed Favre to take his place as head of the little group while he was absent. Favre was to be *como hermano mayor de todos*, not to rule over the others, but to watch over their needs with the affectionate care of an older brother.[33] None of the companions seemed to have objected to this arrangement.

Before he left, Ignatius had arranged to meet the companions in Venice sometime in the spring of 1537 so that the group could take ship together for Palestine. The dream of going to the Holy Land was still alive. During Ignatius's absence, Favre received three more companions into the little group: his old friend from La Roche days, Claude Jay; Jay's classmate in Paris, a priest, Paschase Broët; and Jean Codure, also a priest.[34] All three did the Spiritual Exercises under Favre's direction.

By the spring of 1536, Favre had managed to put aside enough money to take his Master's biretta, and, in April, he became 'Master Pierre'. By the autumn of 1536, all the companions had gained their Master's degrees.

## A time of war

On the larger stage, this was the time of a renewed outbreak of war between Emperor Charles V and Francis I of France. There was the threat of a siege of Paris by the imperial forces. The shadow of this conflict fell over the University of Paris and made it imperative for the subjects of the emperor to think of withdrawing from France. This being the case, Favre and the other companions concluded that it would be better for them to cut short their theological studies in Paris and leave for Venice earlier than the date agreed upon with Ignatius.

**Notes**

1. Humanism was essentially a cultural movement that appealed to classical antiquity as a model of eloquence. The important thing was to return *ad fontes* ('back to the sources').
2. Desiderius Erasmus (1469–1536) was *the* outstanding humanist scholar in Europe of the time.
3. A regent was a young teacher of undergraduate students.
4. Juan de La Peña enrolled at the University of Paris in 1522 (at Sainte Barbe). He received the Master of Arts degree in 1525. He accepted the position of regent, and it was as such that he was a tutor to Favre and Xavier from 1526 onwards, and to Ignatius Loyola from 1529. See Philippe Lécrivain, *Paris in the Time of Ignatius Loyola*, trans. by Ralph C. Renner (St Louis, MO: Institute of Jesuit Sources, 2011), p. 66.

5. See Mary Purcell, *The Quiet Companion* (Dublin: Gill and Macmillan, 1970), p. 32.
6. William of Ockham (c. 1285–1347) was a native of Ockham in Surrey, England. He entered the Franciscan Order and studied and taught at Oxford. He was a philosopher and theologian. He asserted that the universal is not found at all in reality, but only in the human mind, for every substance is radically individual.
7. Scholasticism was the educational tradition of the medieval schools, influenced by the thought of Aristotle. Scholastic theology presented a doctrine in argument, counter-argument and solution. Typical of this approach is the *Summa Theologica* of Thomas Aquinas.
8. Thomas Aquinas (c. 1225–1274) was a Dominican priest, philosopher and theologian. Aquinas was the foremost scholastic thinker.
9. For example, if we have a red car, a red apple, a red flower, the realist will claim that 'redness' is a real universal property; the nominalist will claim that only individual red things exist. For the nominalist, 'redness' is just a name we use to group similar objects.
10. We have only to think of the key importance St Ignatius of Loyola attributes to experience in the *Spiritual Exercises*, especially in the discernment of spirits.
11. Gabriel Biel (1420–1495) was a member of the Brethren of the Common Life as well as being an illustrious theologian.
12. In Bangert, *To the Other Towns*, p. 34.
13. Footnote 47 in *Spiritual Writings of Pierre Favre,* p. 21. These professors were: Jacques Barthélemy, professor at the Sorbonne; Pierre de Cornibus, Franciscan; François Picart and Jean Adam, who taught in the Collège de Navarre; Robert Wauchope, from Sainte Barbe (archbishop of Armagh *in absentia*); Thomas Laurent and Jean Benoit, Dominicans from Saint-Jacques.
14. Lécrivain, *Paris in the Time of Ignatius Loyola*, p. 69.
15. Pedro de Ribadeneira (1527–1611) was born in Toledo, Spain, and entered the Jesuits in 1540. He studied at Paris, Louvain and Padua. He wrote the first biography of Ignatius of Loyola in 1572.
16. See Pedro de Ribadeneira, *The Life of Ignatius of Loyola* (St Louis, MO: The Institute of Jesuit Sources, 2014), p. 99.
17. Juan de Castro (1485–1556) was born in Burgos, Spain and entered the Collège de Coqueret in Paris in 1526. While still a student he made the Spiritual Exercises under Ignatius in 1529. In 1532, he gained his doctorate in theology, returned to Spain and became a Carthusian monk. He died as prior of the Charterhouse of Porta Coeli (Valencia) in 1556.
18. *Memoriale*, 8–12.
19. Ribadeneira, *The Life of Ignatius of Loyola,* p. 111.
20. In *Spiritual Writings of Pierre Favre*, p. 17.
21. Simão Rodrigues (1509–1579) was born in Portugal and joined the companions in Paris in 1533. Ordained in Venice in 1537, he was the first provincial of Portugal and later provincial of Castile, Spain. In 1577, he wrote an account of his Paris days with the companions. He died in Lisbon in 1579.
22. Paschase Broët (1500–1562) was a priest for ten years before joining the companions. He chose Favre as his spiritual director. He came on a brief visit to Ireland in 1541. He became first Jesuit provincial of France.
23. Diego Laínez (1512–1565) was from Castile, Spain and studied in Alcalà and Paris. He joined the companions, and was ordained in Venice in 1537. He was appointed by Pope Paul III as papal theologian at the Council of Trent. He was the second superior general of the Society of Jesus. Alfonso Salmerón (1515–1585) was from Toledo, Spain and joined the companions in Paris. He paid a brief visit to Ireland in 1541 and was a papal theologian at the Council of Trent. He wrote a sixteen-volume commentary on the New Testament. Nicolás Bobadilla (1508–1590) was from Old Castile, Spain and studied at Valladolid, Alcalà and Paris. He joined the companions in Paris, and was ordained in 1537. He was sent on various missions throughout Europe by Pope Paul III.
24. See Joseph de Guibert, *The Jesuits: Their Spiritual Doctrine and Practice* (St Louis, MO: The Institute of Jesuit Sources, 1986), p. 79.
25. Quoted in Joseph F. Conwell, *Walking in the Spirit: A Reflection on Jeronimo Nadal's Phrase 'Contemplative Likewise in Action'* (St Louis, MO: The Institute of Jesuit Sources, 2003), p. 61.
26. *Memoriale*, 14.

27. *Spiritual Writings of Pierre Favre*, p. 67.
28. *Memoriale*, 14.
29. *Memoriale*, 14.
30. The other four companions were Diego Laínez, Alfonso Salmerón, Nicolás Alonso Bobadilla, and Simão Rodrigues.
31. See Joseph F. Conwell, *A Brief and Exact Account: The Recollections of Simão Rodrigues on the Origin and Progress of the Society of Jesus* (St Louis, MO: Institute of Jesuit Sources, 2004), p. 16.
32. Lécrivain, *Paris in the Time of Ignatius Loyola*, pp. 101–102.
33. See John Carroll Futtrell, *Making an Apostolic Community of Love: The Role of the Superior according to St Ignatius of Loyola* (St Louis, MO: The Institute of Jesuit Sources, 1970), p. 24.
34. Jean Codure (1508–1541) was a native of the tiny town of Seyne, high in the Alps. He had already done some theology before he came to Paris. He studied at the Collège Lisieux. He, too, made the Exercises under Favre and, on 15 August 1536, went with Broët and the other companions to Montmartre to join them in their vows, which they renewed on that day. He was confessor to Margaret of Austria, daughter of Charles V. He worked with Ignatius on an early draft of the Jesuit *Constitutions*. He was the first of the early companions to die in 1541.

## Chapter 3

# Venice, Rome and Parma (1537–1540)

### Venice

The companions began their journey on foot to Venice in two groups, one leaving on 11 November and the other on 15 November 1536. On their way, when possible, the four priests among them (Favre, Jay, Broët and Codure) celebrated Mass. When they had to make decisions, they went with the majority opinion in a spirit of concord.[1] It rained continuously while they were in France. The serious possibility of meeting the warring factions in south-eastern France forced them to decide on a less direct route eastward through Champagne, then through Lorraine and Germany into Italy. In a letter from Venice to the confessor of Queen Eleanor of Austria, the wife of Francis I, Ignatius writes of how 'Master Pierre Favre and his little company are likely to have a fairly laborious journey … he and his company will be in considerable or even extreme necessity'.[2]

Notwithstanding the above, their long and exhausting journey of about 800 miles ended on 8 January 1537. The 'little company' arrived in Venice 'safe in body and joyful in spirit'.[3] Favre mentions this journey in the *Memoriale*:

> We travelled on foot, passing through Lorraine and Germany where there were already many Lutheran or Zwinglian towns, such as Basle, Constance … It was very cold and deep winter; besides, France and Spain were at war, but the Lord preserved and delivered us from all these dangers.[4]

Meanwhile, Ignatius had finished his sojourn in Azpetia (the Basque region of Spain) about the end of July 1535 and had been in Venice since the end of December of the same year. There, he continued his theological studies and gave the Spiritual Exercises to a considerable number of people. While awaiting his Paris companions, Ignatius gathered a further three – Diego Hoses, a priest from Malaga in Andalusia, Spain, and two cousins of Francis Xavier, the brothers Estaban and Diego de Eguía. These latter two met Ignatius in Venice on their return from Jerusalem, made the Spiritual Exercises and would later join Ignatius in Rome.

The newly arrived companions went to live and work in the hospitals of Venice, four in the Hospital of Ss John and Paul and five in the Hospital of the Incurables, waiting until Lent before going to Rome. The priests among them were busy hearing confessions and in the ministry of spiritual direction.

## Rome

On 16 March 1537, Ignatius sent his companions to Rome to obtain from Pope Paul III a permit to travel to the Holy Land. They were also to seek permission from the pope for the ordination of the non-priests among them. Ignatius did not travel to Rome. He thought it better not to, as he had had some previous difficulties while in Paris with Pedro Ortiz. Ortiz was now in Rome as ambassador of the Emperor Charles V to the Vatican. Ignatius was also wary of the presence in Rome of Cardinal Gian Pietro Carafa with whom he had some previous differences.[5]

On Palm Sunday, 25 March 1537, the companions walked through the Porta del Popolo into the Eternal City. On Tuesday of Easter Week, 3 April 1537, they were received in audience by Pope Paul III at the Castel Sant'Angelo. Strangely enough, this privilege was obtained through the kind favour of none other than one of the two men whom Ignatius preferred not to meet, Dr Pedro Ortiz.[6] It would seem that this corpulent layman had been impressed by what he had heard about these Masters of Paris and would become one of their greatest supporters.

Pope Paul III (Alessandro Farnese)[7] was a highly intelligent man, anxious for the spiritual revitalisation of the Church, though still prone to nepotism himself. Nevertheless he was curious about these students from Paris. He invited them to engage in theological dispute while he ate his lunch! So impressed was he by the companions' theological knowledge that he granted them the permissions they sought and also gave them a generous financial gift to help them on their way to Jerusalem, should the political and military situation so allow. Other cardinals and nobles, attached to the Vatican, followed Pope Paul's financial gesture.

Nicolás Bobadilla, one of the early companions, in his eighties, recalls that papal audience. Bobadilla recounts how they found themselves surrounded by learned theologians, bishops and cardinals, all of whom put theological questions to them. Paul III was highly impressed by the theological erudition of the companions, and told them that he would grant them whatever they would ask of him. They replied that all they wanted was his blessing and permission to go to the Holy Land and to be ordained by any bishop whatsoever. The pope told the companions that he doubted they would ever get to Jerusalem.[8]

## Ordinations in Venice

The companions returned to Venice in early May and, on the feast of John the Baptist, 24 June 1537, Ignatius, Xavier, Laínez, Codure, Bobadilla and Rodrigues were ordained as priests by Bishop Vincenzo Negusanti. Alfonso Salmerón, not yet twenty-three, could only be ordained deacon – priesthood would follow later.

The newly ordained priests did not say their first Masses immediately but returned to the hospitals of Venice to care for the sick. By the end of July, however, they soon realised that this work was not allowing them time for the recollection they would have wished in preparation for their first Masses. They, therefore, dispersed in groups of twos and threes to spend forty days in solitude and prayer. Ignatius, Laínez and Favre spent this time in an abandoned Hieronymite convent near Vicenza, the others in Padua, Trieste, Bassano and Verona.

While on retreat in Vicenza, Ignatius came down with a fever. Nevertheless when he heard that Simão Rodrigues was seriously ill in Bassano, Ignatius rose from his bed and, together with Favre, made the sixteen-mile journey to Bassano to visit Rodrigues. On the way, Ignatius recovered from his fever and sensed interiorly that Rodrigues's illness would not end in death. He assured Favre of this fact. The two visited Rodrigues. He recovered and Ignatius and Favre returned to their retreat in Vicenza.[9]

This retreat was followed again by several months of pastoral work in and around Venice. It was at this time that the newly-ordained priests celebrated their first Masses, with the exception of Ignatius who waited until Christmas 1538.

Not being able to realise their dream of going to Jerusalem, the companions decided to spread out among the various university cities in northern and central Italy, hoping to encourage some students to join their way of life. If asked who they were, they were to respond that they were of the *Compagnia di Gesù* (the Company of Jesus).[10] In these cities, they taught catechism to the children, helped the sick and dying, engaged in spiritual conversations, gave the Spiritual Exercises, celebrated Masses and heard confessions.

## Back to Rome

In November 1537, Ignatius, Laínez and Favre came to Rome. Contrary to Ignatius's initial fears, they were warmly welcomed again by Dr Ortiz and by a wealthy Roman citizen, Quirino Garzoni. Garzoni lent them his vacant villa. It was no wonder that Ignatius referred to Garzoni as *molto magnifico Signore* ('very generous Lord').

Pope Paul III was anxious to restructure the Pontifical Sapienza University after the Sack of Rome (1527).[11] The Sapienza had been a victim of this destruction. It had been closed by Pope Clement VII (1523–34). Pope Paul was on the watch for professors and, therefore, immediately assigned Favre to teach Scripture and Laínez to teach scholastic theology in the Sapienza. Favre began his lectures in November 1537 and continued them until May 1539.

On 21 April 1538, Easter Sunday, the other companions arrived in Rome from northern and central Italy. On 5 May, the papal legate, Cardinal Vincenzo Carafa,[12] gave them faculties (permission) to preach everywhere, to hear confessions of both men and women, to absolve from certain reserved cases, to distribute communion and to administer the other sacraments.

The companions started preaching on 5 May. They spread out in several different churches throughout Rome. Xavier and Favre worked together at the Church of San Lorenzo in Damaso. Their preaching caused quite a stir among the Roman populace who were used to sermons being preached only during the penitential seasons of Advent and Lent, and rarely outside Rome's primary churches. This preaching was often intense – sermons could last for hours, so long, in fact, that sometimes the preachers would offer an actual intermission to their listeners![13]

Late in November 1538, when all hope of going to Jerusalem had gone forever because of impending wars with the Turks, Pope Paul asked the companions, 'Why are you men so set on going to Jerusalem? You have a truly genuine Jerusalem here in Italy if you are anxious to accomplish some good in God's Church.'[14] As a result, the companions offered themselves unreservedly to Pope Paul for whatever mission he would decide. The pope gladly accepted their offer. Favre remembers:

> In 1538, we offered ourselves as a holocaust to the sovereign pontiff Paul III … holding ourselves ready to set off at his order for the uttermost point of the Indies … For through the voice of his vicar on earth which gives the clearest of calls, Christ thought it good to show us that he was pleased with what we proposed.[15]

Favre interpreted this event as 'a memorable blessing and the quasi-foundation of the Society'.[16]

On 23 November 1538, Favre wrote an interesting letter to Dr Diogo de Gouveia, a native Portuguese and agent for King John III of Portugal. We might remember that Diogo de Gouveia had been rector of the Collège Sainte-Barbe when the companions were in Paris. In February 1538, Gouveia had written to King John urging him to request the services of the companions for missionary work in India. Favre replied in the name of the all the companions:

> Would that we could satisfy you, and satisfy our own hearts as well in their zealous yearning for the same things as you; but for the present something prevents us from responding to the desires of many others as well as to your own. You will understand this from what I now put down. We who have been bound together in this Society have dedicated ourselves to the sovereign pontiff, since he is head of the universal harvest of Christ; in this oblation we have made it clear to him that we are ready for everything that he might decide for us in Christ; if, therefore, he should send us where you are calling us, we shall gladly go there.[17]

In May 1539 Favre and Laínez were sent on their first papal mission. Though he did not know it then, Pierre Favre would never again meet Jean Codure, Paschase Broët, Alfonso Salmeron or his countryman Claude Jay. Never again would he see his roommate of Sainte Barbe, Francis Xavier.

## Parma

The Parma 'legation', as it was called, forming the central section of the Papal States, was strung across northern Italy from Genoa to Venice and was administered by a papal legate, Cardinal Ennio Filonardo.[18] Filonardo, who was dedicated to church reform, asked Pope Paul for 'two priests of reformed life' who, by their preaching, would defend the Catholic faith. Parma was a disturbed and contentious district, rapidly going over to Lutheranism or Calvinism. Favre and Laínez were chosen from among the companions. After almost two weeks on the road with Cardinal Filonardi, Favre and Laínez entered Parma on 1 July 1539.

In Parma, they both preached in Latin, and so it was to a select audience. They gave lectures on Scripture – Laínez in the cathedral and Favre in the Church of San Gervasio e Protasio. They also gave the Spiritual Exercises, which bore great fruit. Their retreatants, in turn, guided others through the Exercises in groups of ten to fourteen. Laínez is reputed to have been the better preacher, but Favre was 'the specialist of the confessional'. His natural gentleness and kindness, his eagerness to put others at their ease, his winning manner and ready sympathy drew many penitents.

In March of 1540, nine months after their arrival, Favre wrote to Ignatius that he was unable to estimate the number of retreatants, so many people were there doing and giving the Exercises. Three months later, Laínez sent a similar report to Ignatius. The council of the city of Parma wrote to Costanza Farnese, niece of Paul III:

> The greater part of the people of Parma are changed in their manner of life to the extent that they go to confession and Holy Communion much more frequently than had been their habit ... The entire city is converted to a religious fidelity more intense than at any time in her past.[19]

Favre spent some time in Brescia, about fifty miles north of Parma. He went to Brescia to be with a young Jesuit recruit, Angelo Paradisi, who was seriously ill. As fate would have it, Francis Xavier arrived in Parma en route to Lisbon just after Favre had left for Brescia. Xavier had debated whether he should await Favre's return, but submitting to the judgement of the Portuguese ambassador Pedro Mascarenhas, he moved on without delay. This was perhaps Favre's last opportunity to see Xavier.

Favre returned to Parma on 16 April and, nine days later, he himself fell ill with fever and, for three months, until the middle of July, was confined to the house of some friends. During Favre's three-month illness, Laínez was the mainstay of the pastoral work in Parma. When Favre had heard that he had just missed Xavier in Parma, he wrote to Ignatius:

> May the Lord by his grace bring it about that if we do not see each other in this world, we may be able to rejoice together in the next over both the separations and the reunions that we experienced here below for Christ alone.[20]

Favre and Laínez remained in Parma until September 1540, engaged in pastoral work, with the aid of Jerónimo Doménech.[21] Thanks to Favre, Laínez and Domenech, several young men from Parma and its environs entered the Society, among them Antonio Criminali,[22] the first Jesuit martyr.

In August 1540, Favre had been ordered by Paul III to accompany Dr Pedro Ortiz on his return to Spain, in the hope of establishing a Jesuit community there. The news of Favre's imminent departure caused consternation in Parma. One noble lady, Jacoba Pallavicino, asked another noble lady, Laura Pallavicino, a relative of Pope Paul III, to use her influence to have Favre left where he was doing so much good. The city fathers of Parma sent two ambassadors, Frederico del Prato and Angelo Cantelli, to Rome with the same request. Favre was embarrassed over this and wrote to Ignatius:

> Five or six days ago Signora Jacoba, learning of my departure for Spain, ran weeping to the lady Laura, one of the most important persons in this city and a relative of the

> pope, imploring her with tears to prevent me from leaving and to write to Cardinal Santi Fiora[23] to obtain from his Holiness to have me left in Parma. She did this without my knowledge. Also, I believe that the city had made similar representations in writing to his Holiness. I assure you that whatever comes of this I had no part in it.[24]

Representations on the part of these nobles of Parma to Paul III were of no avail. Favre was to go to Spain! Faced with the prospects of losing both Favre and Laínez (who was now in Piacenza), these good citizens requested some written instructions from Favre as to how they might continue to live their spiritual lives. In early September, Favre wrote some instructions for them under the title 'Order and Help for Preserving in the True Christian and Spiritual Life'.

The following are just some of the instructions that Favre gives (dated 7 September 1540):

- One should receive the Sacraments of the Eucharist and Reconciliation at least once a week. It would be good to determine which day of the week this would be.
- One should have a fixed confessor.
- There are further instructions as to morning and night prayers; Examination of Conscience; works of mercy; reflection on the Four Last Things (death, judgement, heaven, hell). Through these spiritual practices, Favre wrote, one will grow in such virtues as humility, patience, prudence, in the knowledge and love of God and in the love of neighbour.

Favre signs this instruction 'Your brother and spiritual father in Christ Jesus, Don Pietro Fabro'.[25] Today's reader may find the instruction to reflect on the Four Last Things as being rather gruesome and depressing, but it was a common spiritual exercise at the time, recommended consistently, through many centuries. Many books were written on the theme of dying well.[26]

## The colloquy in Worms

Pedro Ortiz seems to be crop up continually in our story thus far. We have seen that Favre was to accompany Ortiz to Spain. Ortiz was making his way from Rome to Parma to meet up with Favre when he suddenly received a change of orders from Charles V. Instead of going to Spain, Ortiz and Favre were to travel to Worms in Germany! It so happened that arrangements had been made for the holding a colloquy between Catholic and Protestant theologians in the city of Worms. Charles V commanded Ortiz to attend this gathering as his representative rather than going to Spain, bringing Favre along as a member of his household.

Favre left Parma at the beginning of October, met Ortiz and his retinue at Piacenza, and rode with them to Worms, reaching there on 24 October 1540, the feast of St Raphael the Archangel.

**Notes**

1. Ribadeneira, *The Life of Ignatius of Loyola*, p. 124.
2. Quoted in Javier Osuna, *Friends in the Lord*, trans. by Nicholas King (Way Books, 1970).
3. Quoted in Bangert, *To the Other Towns*, p. 62.
4. *Memoriale*, 16.
5. Gian Pietro Carafa (the future Pope Paul IV) was the founder of the Theatine Order. He was suspicious of Ignatius who presumed to give spiritual direction, and he not even a priest! Ignatius had also presumed to advise Carafa about the lifestyle of the Theatines. Such advice was not welcomed by Carafa.
6. Dr Pedro Ortiz (c. 1500–1548) was a Spanish layman and a member of the theological faculty of Paris. Ortiz occupied the chair of Scripture in Salamanca University. On coming to Rome, he acquired great authority at the papal court as secretary to Pope Clement VIII and as counsellor to Pope Paul III. He did the Spiritual Exercises under Ignatius at the Benedictine monastery of Monte Cassino during Lent of 1538 and became a great supporter of the new Society of Jesus. Later, he was a special ambassador of the Emperor Charles V to the Holy See. While he was studying in Paris, Ignatius had run into certain difficulties with Ortiz. Ortiz objected to Ignatius recruiting some of the academically brightest students at the Montaigu to a new way of life.
7. Pope Paul III (Alessandro Farnese) was born in 1468. In 1493, Pope Alexander VI made him a cardinal at the age of twenty-five, and he was also given a bishopric though he was not yet ordained! By the time he was given the Diocese of Parma, he had fathered three sons and one daughter. By 1519, his life had taken a new turn. On 26 June, he was ordained priest and consecrated bishop two days later. Henceforth his moral conduct was without reproach. He was elected pope in 1534. Right from the beginning, he desired a general council for the reform of the Church. His love of the Church did not transform his love of family. He appointed two of his grandsons, Alessandro Farnese and Guido Sforza, to be cardinals when they were both in their early teens! It is surely remarkable that this is the man to whom, with all his faults, the early companions offered the 'holocaust' of their lives with enthusiasm and love.

8. Quoted in Joseph F. Conwell, *Impelling Spirit: Revisiting a Founding Experience: 1539 Ignatius of Loyola and His Companions* (Chicago: Loyola Press, 1997), p. 37.
9. See Conwell, *Impelling Spirit*, p. 63.
10. Quoted in Spadaro, *Pietro Favre*, p. 42.
11. The forces of the Emperor Charles V engaged in an orgy of destruction and massacre in Rome on 6 May 1527.
12. Cardinal Vincenzo Carafa (1477–1541) was made a cardinal-priest by Pope Clement VIII in 1527. He was *camerlengo* of the College of Cardinals from 1533–34. He died in Naples in 1541. The *camerlengo* is the cardinal who takes over the day-to-day running of the Vatican after the death of a pope, that is, until the new pope is elected in the conclave.
13. John W. O'Malley, *The First Jesuits* (Cambridge, MA: Harvard University Press, 1993), p. 92.
14. Quoted in Bangert, *To the Other Towns*, p. 77.
15. *Memoriale*, 18.
16. Bangert, *To the Other Towns*, p. 77.
17. Quoted in Conwell, *Impelling Spirit*, p. 119.
18. Cardinal Ennio Filonardo (1466–1549) acted as papal nuncio to Switzerland and became cardinal-bishop of Albano in 1546.
19. Quoted in Bangert, *To the Other Towns*, p. 91.
20. Quoted in Bangert, *To the Other Towns*, p. 96.
21. Jerónimo Doménech (1516–1592) was born in Valencia, Spain. He was already a priest when he met Favre in Parma in 1539. He made the Spiritual Exercises under Favre and was accepted into the Society in the same year.
22. Antonio Criminali (1520–1549) was an Italian missionary, beheaded by a local army on the Fishery Coast, India in 1549. He was the protomartyr of the Society of Jesus.
23. The cardinal referred to in Favre's letter was Cardinal Guido Ascania Sforza (1518–1564), eldest son of Cosanza Farnese and, therefore, grandson of Pope Paul III.
24. Quoted in Purcell, *The Quiet Companion*, pp. 72–73.
25. *Spiritual Writings of Pierre Favre*, pp. 321–323.
26. An example of this genre is a work entitled *De arte bene moriendi* written by the Jesuit cardinal Robert Bellarmine (1542–1621).

## Chapter 4

# Worms, Cologne and Portugal (1540–1545)

The city of Worms was a stronghold of Lutheranism. The points that the Lutherans would debate with the Catholic theologians at the colloquy in Worms were justification by faith alone (not by our own works, the stance of Martin Luther); rejection of the Mass, purgatory, pilgrimages, relics, indulgences and invocation of the saints; abolition of monasteries and convents and denial that the papacy was of divine institution – these were the requirements of the Reformers. This must have been very difficult for Favre. He had been trained from childhood to practise good works. He was intensely devoted to the Mass, our Lady, the angels and saints, a fervent pilgrim, an inveterate if not very critical venerator and collector of relics, a friend of Carthusians monks and a staunch upholder of the papacy.

The Colloquy of Worms opened on 25 November. Cardinal Gasparo Contarini[1] objected to Ortiz's being present. Seemingly Ortiz had a short fuse. So explosive was he in debate that Contrarini feared he would wreck any chance of agreement at Worms the moment he opened his mouth.

In a letter to Ignatius dated 27 December 1540, Favre writes:

> In Worms Lutheran doctrine continues to be preached openly in the Dominican church ... Would to God there were in each town of this land two of three priests not

> living openly with women or guilty of other notorious sins. If there were, I feel sure that, with God's help, the ordinary people would turn back. I speak of the towns and cities from which church rule has not yet been totally expelled. The citizens are deceived not so much by the seeming good and preaching of the Lutherans as by the bad example of their own pastors.[2]

While he was in Worms, Favre was engaged in his usual pastoral activities – giving the Spiritual Exercises, hearing confessions and giving spiritual direction.

The Colloquy of Worms broke up without agreement on 18 January 1541. The Protestant side was united, the Catholic quite divided. Favre quickly realised that conferences, colloquies and diets could not bring religious peace. They were open to power politics and to manipulation for purely secular aims.[3]

Favre's eyes were soon opened to the harsh realities at Worms. He painted a grim picture in a letter to Ignatius:

> I am convinced that not a single Lutheran from Worms or any place else has been converted from his errors through the efforts of those who are gathered here for that precise purpose. In other words, I see no fruit that has been gained so far as the conversion of the Lutherans is concerned. In fact, it is clear that they are the ones who are gaining ground, even over those who have come here as professed Catholics … I have not spoken with Melanchthon[4] or any of the other Lutherans. Many of the doctors [theologians] would like me to have a talk with him, and I certainly have had many holy desires to do so … Dr Ortiz … would like to see me in touch with the Lutherans, realising, as he does, that, with the help of God our Lord, I would not debate with them in a contentious spirit, nor would I by nettling them block the hoped for good.[5]

It was proposed, at one stage, by some of the Catholic party at Worms that Favre might meet Philip Melanchthon. Favre wrote about this proposal to Rome:

> Many of the theologians are very anxious for me to have a talk with Melanchthon. They say it would be fitter for me to meet than others who are more punctilious ... Indeed, I have felt many holy desires arise in my soul to do this; yet I do not wish to oppose the judgement of those who are in charge of the colloquy. They do not want anyone to converse with the Lutherans, in case the business which brought us here be impeded. For the same reason, Dr Ortiz has held me back [from meeting Melanchthon] although he himself would like to meet the Lutherans. He knows that with God's help I would not approach them in the spirit of contradiction, nor would I exasperate anyone, or in any way obstruct the business that has brought us here. I have not conversed with Melanchthon or any other Lutheran. I have quite enough to do to live up to my vocation among the Catholics.[6]

This letter reveals some further sides to Favre: the high opinion in which he was held personally by the Catholic side at Worms; the Catholic party must have also held a high opinion of Favre's theological knowledge (although Favre himself would never have claimed to be an academic theologian); also that attractive side to Favre's character, that ability to engage in respectful dialogue with anyone, without fear of intimidating them or causing any rancour; again there is that self-deprecating tendency that we have already noted in Favre's character. In all of this, we find echoes of what Pope Francis said about Favre in that interview with Spadaro in 2013.

Whether or not Favre actually met with Melanchthon is open to question. The fact that such an encounter is not mentioned in

Favre's *Memoriale* is no proof that such a meeting did not take place. We will see later that the Jesuit Peter Canisius, in a letter to Ignatius, writes of Favre debating with another reformer, Martin Bucer,[7] in Bonn.

It seems that Favre's letters to Rome were not as frequent as Ignatius would have wished. Ignatius insisted that he wanted to be kept abreast of the religious situation in Germany. Favre admitted his negligence in writing letters but then wrote of the gloomy prospects for the success of the colloquy:

> The Protestants tell us that their purpose is simply the reformation of the Church, and they make this assertion in such a convincing way that ignorant and stupid people believe them even when they see them desecrating statues, overturning altars – save one in each church – blaspheming those who hear private Masses or pray to the saints ... To see the blindness that had befallen this nation is something to arouse the fear of Christ our Lord ... The aim of the Protestants is to leave not a stone upon a stone ... their supreme desire being ... to cause irreparable cleavage in Holy Mother Church, against which, however, not even the gates of hell will ever prevail.[8]

Favre rapidly came to the conclusion at Worms that any hope for the Roman Catholic Church in Germany lay in a return to a life of prayer, of fidelity to the sacraments, of the practice of charity. He also believed that it was not so much the doctrines of Luther as the bad example of the priests that was causing the defection of so many people. Favre was looking at Germany more through the eyes of a shepherd of souls than those of a theological disputant.

One of the most famous Roman Catholic theologians whom Favre met in Worms was John Cochlaeus.[9] Cochlaeus became one of Favre's great admirers, and, on one occasion, when he heard Favre speak of the difference between the knowledge of spiritual things and the taste for them, he remarked, 'I am delighted that at last we have discovered a master of the affective life.' Cochlaeus wanted to do the Spiritual Exercises with Favre there and then but Favre was due to leave Worms for Regensburg by way of Speyer.

The journey to Speyer and Regensburg was occasioned by the breakdown of the discussions between the Catholic and the Lutherans in Worms and, consequently, Charles V was forced to adjourn the colloquy to Regensburg (Ratisbon) where he could be present in person and make efforts to restore religious peace in Germany.

## Speyer and Regensburg (Ratisbon)

From Worms, Favre journeyed south to Speyer where he was received by the local bishop and by other distinguished guests, both clerical and lay. He left Speyer on 6 February and reached Regensburg on the day of the emperor's arrival there on 23 February. The Diet of Regensburg began in early April 1541.[10]

The emperor's programme called for moderate and restrained disputants, from both the Catholic and Protestant sides. The early discussions on original sin and free will were going well but certain difficulties arose, not insurmountable, with the question of justification. However when the subject of the Eucharist came up for discussion, the Lutherans[11] denied the Roman Catholic teaching on transubstantiation.[12] Agreement could not be reached, especially on this issue, and so, the diet floundered.

While in Regensburg, Favre was finally able to give the Spiritual Exercises to John Cochlaeus. Cochlaeus, in turn, gave the Exercises to others. Another champion of the Exercises was to be Robert Wauchope, archbishop of Armagh.[13] He, too, became an apostle of the Exercises.

It is interesting that Favre seems to have done very little preaching while in Regensburg. He appears to have had a certain diffidence with regard to his preaching abilities. He wrote to Ignatius:

'I do no preaching lest my growing influence among the gentlemen here in the confessional and in private conversation suffer as a consequence.'[14]

Favre was the master of spiritual conversation and direction. Again, perhaps, there is a sign of Favre's self-deprecating humour in the above quotation.

Favre pronounced his solemn vows of religious profession as a Jesuit at the high altar in the church known as Alte Kapelle in Regensburg, on the feast of the Visitation 1541. His vows were of chastity, poverty and obedience to the superior general of the new Society of Jesus (Ignatius Loyola). Favre also took a fourth vow of obedience to the pope with regard to missions (to go wherever he might be sent by the pope).[15] He sent three copies of these vows to Ignatius in Rome, three for safety's sake, the mail being uncertain in those times.

During all this time in Regensburg, Favre was in the company of Pedro Ortiz. Mary Purcell, in *The Quiet Companion*, tells us that two more opposite temperaments than those of Pedro Ortiz and Favre it would be difficult to imagine:

> Ortiz, the extrovert, self-confident, flamboyant, fond of the limelight, easily aroused to fury, not caring whose corns he trod on, plebian or imperial, Lutheran or Catholic and Favre the introvert, diffident, self-effacing, gentle, fearful of hurting anyone's feelings.[16]

Favre wrote to Ignatius from Regensburg:

> The doctor [Pedro Ortiz] is preaching before the emperor, without as much as one rehearsal or any practice in the neighbourhood or to any congregation less than Caesar's [Charles V's] court. Each day, indeed, he increases not in wisdom and age but in vehemence and volume. His hearers shake in their shoes. Praised be to God for all his gifts and mercies![17]

And a fortnight later:

> The doctor continues to preach, giving several sermons each week ... He is now so eager for the pulpit that he is not at all pleased with those who listen to him only once a day. His sermons bear such fruit that all marvel. I do not preach for fear of losing what reputation I have as a confessor and director ... I made threats to many people that if no other preacher could be found I myself would mount the pulpit and preach. They soon arranged for three to preach before his Majesty, Dr Ortiz, Fray Alonso and another Augustinian.[18]

Here, is a fine example of Favre's charitable insight into Ortiz and, again, into that self-deprecating humour. So while Ortiz addressed the Emperor Charles and his court twice daily, Favre heard confessions, engaged in spiritual direction and gave the Exercises. He recalls:

> Our Lord granted me the grace to accomplish some remarkable things in his service, especially in the confessions of many noblemen of the imperial court or the court of my prince, the duke of Savoy who had chosen me as his personal confessor ... Much seed was sown for the still greater good which resulted from them. And the same is true of the Exercises made by important persons, Spaniards and Italians as well as Germans, all very influential. From these Exercises there resulted almost all the good that has been done since then in Germany.[19]

From Regensburg, writing to the scholastics (Jesuits in training) in Paris on 12 May 1541, Favre comments that

> mere learning is so ineffective against the heretics. With the world having reached such a state of unbelief, what

> are needed are arguments of deeds and of blood; otherwise, things will only get worse and error will increase. Words and reasons are no longer sufficient to convince heretics, in Ratisbon or anywhere else.[20]

Favre does not appear to have studied the works of the reformers – in Germany, Catholics were forbidden to read their writings. He was so immersed in pastoral work that he could spare little time for study. His primary aim was the reform of monasteries and convents, the spiritual renewal of the clergy and the formation of a Catholic laity well grounded in their faith. His choice of retreatants (mostly clergy and religious) indicates the main thrust of his pastoral campaign: reform the pastors and the pastors, in turn, will reform their people. Once a priest had been formed by the Exercises, that same priest might give the Exercises to others.

Favre always distinguished between the full Spiritual Exercises (of thirty days) and shorter, more flexible forms, consisting essentially of the First Week[21] and a general confession. The effects of the Exercises on the retreatants were said to be miraculous: bishops and abbots began to reform their dioceses or their monasteries; crowds of students became Carthusians, Franciscans or Jesuits; noblemen changed their way of life. Perhaps there is some hyperbole here, nevertheless, Favre's pastoral strategy always consisted of 'confessions, conversations and the Exercises' – his customary description of his ministry. His accustomed ministry bore much fruit.

Mary Purcell, however, tells us that the Lutheran leaders at Regensburg were far ahead of the Catholics as propagandists and publicists.[22] The Catholic theologians wrote treatises in Latin for perusal by theologians on the other side. Too late did the Catholics realise what the Lutherans had known all along – the importance of simple-worded, direct, forceful pamphlets, written in the vernacular so that everyone could understand.

## A visit to Villaret and on to Spain

Cardinal Contarini, who had come to Regensburg with high hopes, reported to Rome in June that his soul was in anguish at seeing things moving so fast on the road to ruin.[23] In July 1541 the diet at Regensburg collapsed over questions concerning the sacraments, transubstantiation and the authority of the pope.

With the collapse of the diet, Favre and Ortiz were now free to resume their journey to Spain, which had been postponed because of the order to attend Worms and Regensburg. So, at the end of July, Favre left Regensburg for Spain with Ortiz and another Jesuit or lay companion, whose identity is unknown.

On the way, having passed through Bavaria and the Swiss cantons, they made a short stay in Savoy. Favre spent six days with his relatives at Villaret. Many years after his death, witnesses came forward in 1596 and again in 1607 to speak about Favre's short visit. They recounted how he taught them to say the Rosary. He encouraged them to wear rosary beads on their belts as a way of professing their Catholic faith openly. He preached in the church where he had been baptised, St-Jean-de-Sixt, and in the church of Grand-Bornand, which was larger.[24] One local lady of the time recalled Favre's home visit, describing him as 'wonderfully attractive, humble, grave, eloquent and very learned'.

It is likely that Favre would have visited his first cousin, Dom Claude Périssen, prior of the Carthusian Monastery of Le Reposoir. Two witnesses at the 1596 enquiry stated that Favre's brother petit-Louis complained to him of his harsh lifestyle and poverty, as he, a poor farmer, struggled on the mountains.

Favre's stay was brief. On their way to Lyons, near Nantua, Favre, Ortiz and their fellow travellers were arrested by some French soldiers who were suspicious of them since most of them were Spaniards. They were held captive for seven days. In the *Memoriale*, Favre thanks the Lord for their eventual release:

> The great favour conferred on us there by our Lord should never be forgotten. In his goodness he delivered us from our captors and granted us so much grace for conversing with them and benefiting their souls that their captain sought confession and confessed to me.[25]

Favre even speaks of 'feelings of warm friendship' that grew between the small group of travellers and their captors.

Eventually, on crossing the Spanish border, Favre would typically invoke the protection of the archangels, the angel guardians and the saints of Spain.[26] The group made their way to the Benedictine monastery of Montserrat, near Barcelona. From Montserrat they rode via Saragossa and Alcalá, arriving in Madrid on 27 October 1541.

Pedro Ortiz, though a doctor of theology, was not an ordained priest. Nevertheless he held a benefice[27] in the surrounding district of Galapagar, north-west of Madrid. He paid a priest to care for the parish. Ortiz asked Favre to minister in the Galapagar region, which he willingly did in the months of November and December. Favre was to be seen every afternoon at about two o'clock teaching prayers and catechism to nearly a hundred little boys and girls, on occasion adults, even priests, joined them. He also gave the Exercises in various forms.

No sooner had Favre arrived in Spain, however, than there came a letter, dated 22 December 1541, from Cardinal Farnese[28] in Rome, on behalf of the pope, summoning Favre back to Germany. He was to join two other Jesuits, Nicolas Bobadilla and Claude Jay, as advisors to Cardinal Morone[29] in drawing up proposals for the Council of Trent. Favre received this letter sometime in January 1542 while he was in Ocaña at the royal court of the infantas (royal princesses) Maria and Juana, daughters of Emperor Charles V.

Favre visited these young princesses at the instruction of Ortiz. What the purpose of the visit was is not clear, since Maria was only thirteen and Juana six! However Favre did want to see his friend Ferdinand de Silva, count of Cifuentes, who resided at the royal court. Favre preached to the great ladies of the royal household. When he left Ocaña, the infantas sent their two chaplains, Juan de Aragon and Alvaro Alfonso,[30] to accompany him as far as Toledo. Ortiz was already in Toledo, awaiting Favre's arrival. There they bade farewell to the two chaplains.

The papal nuncio to Spain, following instructions from Rome, told Favre to proceed to Barcelona and from there to Speyer in Germany where Cardinal Morone would assign him duties. On his way to Barcelona, Favre made a detour to visit the parents and sisters of Diego Laínez. Ortiz had parted from Favre in February 1542. Further on in his journey, Favre was overtaken by the two chaplains from Ocaña. They had been so impressed by Favre that they had returned to the infantas and asked and obtained permission to leave the royal court and follow him.

Favre and his two new disciples reached Barcelona on 15 March 1542. In Barcelona, this group of travellers was received hospitably by the viceroy of Catalonia and his wife. Later, as a widower, this viceroy would become a Jesuit and would be known to posterity as St Francis Borgia, the third superior general of the Society of Jesus. It seems that Borgia was very much taken with Favre and opened his heart and soul to him.

Favre thanked God that on this long and perilous journey from Spain to Germany the group was preserved from all temporal misfortunes, such as brigands in Catalonia, imprisonment in France, soldiers on their crossing from Savoy into Switzerland and heretics in Germany. He was especially grateful that God preserved the small group from temptations that divide, meaning the spirit of division. They were only human after all. There must have been tensions among them as they walked along the road! Nevertheless Favre recounts how during that journey our Lord gave him many feelings of love and hope for 'heretics' and for the whole world.[31]

## Speyer

Favre reached Speyer in the Rhineland of Germany on 14 April 1542. On his arrival, he found that Cardinal Morone and the Jesuits Nicolas Bobadilla and Claude Jay had just left for other work! Jay had gone to Regensburg; Bobadilla to Vienna; Cardinal Morone to other German towns, prior to his returning to Rome to receive his cardinal's red hat. Morone left instructions that Favre was to consider himself free to undertake whatever work God might inspire him to do until further orders from either Ignatius, the pope or Morone himself. In a letter to Ignatius Loyola, dated 27 April 1542, written from Speyer, Favre berates himself for having arrived there late:

> If those who sent me to Germany had written to me that I should be in Speyer, or wherever the cardinal of Modena [Morone] was staying, on such and such a day under holy obedience, I would have managed and found a way to carry it out to the letter. But being told just to do what I could to get here, I was left so low in strength and faith that all I could find out to manage or manage to find out was to arrive belatedly, as I did, and after the cardinal of Modena's departure from Speyer, on Saturday after the feast of the Resurrection – a piece of news that for me had more of the Passion than of the Resurrection to it.[32]

It would seem that Favre had written to Ignatius just the week before giving much the same news. He writes now because

> I then failed to make clear the great longing I necessarily have for your [Ignatius's] letters – the reason being so that I can learn what I ought to do. For you know the difference between being moved by oneself and being moved by holy obedience, which, in a word, is consummate counsel, true prudence, utter discretion, strength

> and charity for whoever accepts it with perfect humility, patience and joy.[33]

It is interesting to see here Favre's lack of self-confidence and his need to be directed by a higher authority so that he can be assured that he is doing God's will. He feels that Cardinal Morone had given him too much freedom of choice. In the meantime, however, Favre was not idle in Speyer. He was giving the Spiritual Exercises to the two former royal chaplains, Juan de Aragón and Alvaro Alfonso, to the vicar general of the diocese and to Bishop Otto Truchsess.[34] Favre thanked God that he had no lack of harvest to keep him busy.

Initially Favre, Juan de Aragón and Alvaro Alfonso were treated with suspicion by some of the Catholic clergy and people of Speyer. They were thought to be spies of the nuncio, Morone, seeking out in different places the wicked secrets of the city and of the clergy so as to write to the pope.[35] Gradually Favre's gentle, attractive nature wore down the barriers of suspicion and, within a month, many people, especially priests, were coming to him for confession and the Exercises.

The two former royal chaplains completed the Exercises and had become Jesuit novices, doing their novitiate under Favre's guidance. He sent both of them on pilgrimage – Juan de Aragón to visit the shrine of the Three Kings (the Magi) at Cologne[36] and Alvaro Alfonso to Trier to venerate the Holy Shroud.[37] They were each sent out alone and penniless – they were to trust totally in providence for their food and accommodation.

While the two novices were absent, Favre paid a brief visit to Albert of Brandenberg, the cardinal-archbishop of Mainz. This was the same Albert who had delegated the Dominican friar John Tetzel, way back in 1517, to preach the special indulgence that provoked Martin Luther to nail his ninety-five theses to the door of the university church in Wittenberg.

One of the tasks Cardinal Albert assigned to Favre was to review certain writings that he felt might be injurious to the faithful of his diocese. We do not know what these writings were. As an expression of gratitude for his services, Albert presented Favre with a valuable silver vase. Favre politely refused it, explaining that he was not quite accustomed to carrying silverware around with him!

## The Memoriale

In Speyer, on 15 June 1542, in his thirty-sixth year, Favre set about writing his spiritual journal, his *Memoriale*. Mary Purcell gives an accurate and sensitive description of the purpose of the *Memoriale*:

> He began it to remind himself of the favours he had received during life and for which he owed God thanks. Its opening pages are strewn with the phrases 'Recall, O my soul' and 'O my soul, remember.' Further on, the journal serves a different purpose. After prayer and meditation, Favre would jot down the thoughts that came to him and analyse the effects these thoughts had had upon him, whether they brought consolation, enlightenment and peace of mind or caused him discouragement, sadness and loss of tranquility.
>
> Then, Favre applied the Ignatian rules for discerning the source of these thoughts and judged whether they were temptations, autosuggestions or the promptings of the Holy Spirit. Thus, the *Memoriale* became for him an instrument for discovering the will of God in his regard, a help to decide – in the light of that discovery – what to undertake and what to relinquish. The entries, made almost daily for over a year, later became intermittent; they map his spiritual ascent. Favre's early and unexpected death revealed what was obviously intended for no eyes but his own … the author's dialogue with his own soul, a dialogue too intimate and sacred to admit of any listener but God.[38]

The greater part of the *Memoriale* was written in one year, from June 1542 to July 1543. Favre's purpose was spiritual clarification; he concentrated his attention on his interior life. Favre first recorded his life up to June 1542, so that he could recall in a spirit of thanksgiving the blessings he had received from God; the entries that then follow show him absorbed in the study of his inner experience, intent upon finding the will of God. Writing day after day, he completed the bulk of the work in one year. In July 1543, he left for Cologne and gave up keeping the journal until January 1545, when he began the few final pages covering five months.

## Mainz

With the exception of thirteen days spent in Mainz from 15–28 September 1542, Favre remained in Speyer until October. The nuncio, Morone, had instructed him to visit Mainz where Cardinal Albert, archbishop-elector of Brandenburg,[39] was also concerned about the low spiritual and moral state of his clergy.

Favre made such a deep impression on the Cardinal Albert that he was ordered to return to Mainz with his two priest-novices. He arrived there from Speyer about 20 October. The cardinal had expressed the desire that, in his name, Favre should go with his other delegates to the Council of Trent, due to begin on 1 November. The cardinal's request had plunged Favre into an experience of contradictory spiritual movements: joy and sorrow, consolation and desolation. He could not decide what he should do. God then gave him grace to make an act of total abandonment in blind obedience:

> But the Lord delivered me from all of them [different movements] by virtue of a holy and blind obedience which does not take into account either my personal insufficiency or the magnitude and gravity of what has been imposed on me.[40]

In a letter to Ignatius, dated 7 November, Favre writes that

> although I have shown my little competence for a matter of such importance, [the cardinal] has decided that I go along with some of his scholars to the Council, for which he has ordered me to get ready.[41]

Here, we see something of the diffident Favre, initially thinking himself unequal to the proposed task, but then he is given the grace to trust in blind obedience to him whom he now considers to be his legitimate religious superior – Cardinal Albert. Ironically the cardinal later countermanded the order and told Favre that he was to continue a series of lectures on Scripture that he was giving and was to preach in Latin every Sunday.[42]

By a further command of the cardinal of Mainz, Favre gave the Exercises and a series of lectures on the Psalms to the theological faculty of the University of Mainz. He attracted three times more listeners than did the ordinary lecturers at the university. He attributes his success here to the effect of mystical grace he had received. Before that, he felt that he lacked coherence; his memory was faulty; he found it difficult to memorise and suffered from nervousness.[43]

Favre walked the city of Mainz begging alms for the sick and poor. He started a hostel for needy pilgrims and travellers and a house for the sick poor. He was often in financial straits.[44] He was responsible now for the support of Juan de Aragón, Alvaro Alfonso and Esteban Carola (a novice from Speyer).[45]

Favre was absent from Mainz from 28/29 December to 13/14 January on a visit to Cardinal Albert at his residence in Aschaffenburg, about forty miles east of Mainz. The cardinal received him warmly and ordered that his personal collection of relics be laid out for Favre to view in his private chapel.

Favre, who generally accepted without question the authenticity of all relics, was initially greatly impressed. However this time he may have detected illusion somewhere in the brilliant display he saw in the cardinal's chapel:

> On the octave of St Stephen, I said Mass in the chapel of the lord archbishop of Mainz, which for my sake had been splendidly adorned with all his relics and treasures. The day after … I said Mass in the cathedral in another chapel reserved for the lord archbishop; it too was splendidly adorned … at the altar itself, I was in a state of almost total aridity, and this state lasted until the end of Mass. Then it happened that a grace from Christ crucified deprived me completely of any longing I had to seek in these outward shows a means either of increasing interior devotion or of finding Christ crucified with more success … I experienced then in my soul a certain shrinking from the favour of men and the patronage to be obtained from the great.[46]

Martin Luther certainly would have had no doubts but that such relics were fakes! Luther wrote sarcastically that typically among such displays were 'a fine piece of the left horn of Moses and three flames from the bush of Moses on Mount Sinai, each indulged by the pope'.[47]

Up to the beginning of April 1543, Favre had been lodging with the parish priest of St Christopher's in Mainz, a man named 'the reverend Conrad'. Favre had converted this priest from a life of concubinage. Conrad was later to enter the Charterhouse in Cologne.

Favre rented a house in Mainz from 1 April. On moving in, before entering every room and passage, he knelt down and said a prayer, praying that the house be delivered from evil spirits. Seemingly this house was in a disreputable neighbourhood where the spirit of fornication haunted the prostitutes and adulterers of the vicinity. Beside the house was a ruined chapel, defiled by the acts of fornication committed by people who passed through it. Favre mentions his great longings to restore this chapel.[48] For him, the ruins of the chapel were symbolic not only of material ruin but also of spiritual ruin in the area. He would stay in this rented house until his final departure from Mainz.

One of the first who came to stay in the newly rented house was a young Fleming named Peter Canisius.[49] Canisius was already a Master of Arts and was now doing the last of a three-year theology course in Cologne University. Favre had sent the novice-priest Alvaro Alfonso to study at Cologne where, in about January 1543, he met Canisius. So Canisius heard about the new order of priests from Alfonso. Canisius was eager to meet Favre and decided to visit Mainz. Canisius was friendly with the Carthusians in Cologne. His friend Dom Gerhard Kalkbrenner,[50] prior of the Carthusians in Cologne, had also heard of Favre and encouraged Canisius to go to Mainz, giving him a letter inviting Favre to Cologne.

Canisius came to Mainz around 10 April and was soon doing the Spiritual Exercises under Favre's direction. In response to Dom Gerhard's invitation to come to Cologne, Favre wrote on 12 April 1543:

> As for the pilgrimage [to Cologne] which your Paternity urges upon me, I am at present in no position to say what I will be doing in the near future. Meanwhile I shall take advantage of the company of Master Peter [Canisius], which brings me more enjoyment than I can possibly express. Blessings upon him who planted this well-grown tree; blessings upon those who in anyway watered it – I do not doubt that a share in this my blessings falls to your Paternity, who in so many ways wrought upon this young man to be what he is.[51]

On 8 May 1543, in Favre's presence, Canisius took a vow to enter the Society of Jesus. It was Canisius's twenty-second birthday. He wrote to the Carthusians in Cologne:

> Favourable, in every sense of the word, was the wind that brought me to Mainz. I found, to my great profit, the man I sought – if he is a man and not an angel of God. I have never met a more learned or profound theologian, or a man of such lofty and unique sanctity ... He is so highly esteemed here that a number of religious, bishops and theologians have taken him as their spiritual director ... Thanks to him and no one else several priests and ecclesiastics have sent away their concubines, renounced worldly ways, broken with vice and are now living holy lives. As for me, I cannot say how completely those Exercises have changed my soul and my opinions, enlightened my mind ... and revigorated my will.[52]

One finds it hard to accept the judgement of Canisius that Favre was such a brilliant theologian. Though Favre was intelligent, he was not an intellectual. He was essentially a pastoral theologian, whose first and last interest was to bring people to a true conversion of heart.[53]

Around this time, Favre recalls the many different lodgings in which he had stayed during his lifetime. He reflects that his life, up to this time, has been a wandering and restless one – 'as I reflect God intended it to be'.[54] Over the years, he found himself frequently in places threatened by all kinds of diseases:

> I very often spent the night in filthy hospitals,[55] often again in wretched lodgings, at times in bitter cold and in places destitute of everything except a roof, hay and straw. And, on occasion, I even had to sleep in the open air.[56]

In another place, Favre writes of his being exposed to the danger of robbers, of war, of epidemics, especially in Germany; the danger of wild beasts in the forests, danger of spies, of famine, of thirst, of beds infected with lice. In Savoy, there was the danger of brigands dressed as pilgrims, kidnapping wealthy people and demanding ransom for their release.[57] Favre's constant travels in mission obviously demanded physical stamina, courage and total trust in divine providence.

On 28 May 1543, Favre wrote to his Carthusian cousin, Dom Claude Périssin, the prior of Le Reposoir in Savoy, telling him that he has made the acquaintance of the Carthusians of Mainz and sometimes retires from his work in the city to spend a few quiet days with them. He further writes:

> Some days ago, the prior of the Cologne Chartreuse wrote urging me to visit that city, three days journey from here. His letter states that Cologne is in dire straits, so I mean to go there provided that the cardinal of Mainz, expected back soon, agrees.[58]

The cardinal agreed, and to Cologne Favre went!

## Cologne

During August 1543, Favre left Mainz for Cologne. It seems that the position of the Church in Cologne was growing more and more critical. Dom Gerhard Kalkbrenner wrote again and again, as did Canisius, begging Favre to come to Cologne. Eventually, a message came to Favre from the clergy, university and civic leaders of Cologne entreating him to come. Favre's task would be to sustain the Catholics of Cologne and their leaders in a campaign of resistance to the Lutheranising efforts of their cardinal archbishop, Hermann von Wied.

Wied had been planning reform in his diocese for years. But a more unlikely reformer could not be imagined. As a man he was an enigma; as a theologian, an ignoramus. It is said that he had been described by a member of his household as 'very fond of hunting and not particularly well educated'.[59] It is difficult to detect in him a single quality that might have made him a spiritual leader. 'Neither a Protestant nor a Catholic but a proper heathen,' growled Emperor Charles V. Charles also asked, 'How would the good man go about doing any reforming? His knowledge of Latin is nil, and during his long life he has not celebrated Mass more than three times. He does not even know the *confiteor*.'[60]

Wied turned to the Lutherans for advice about reform in his diocese. They advised him that only Martin Bucer and Philip Melanchthon were fit to plan and carry out the reformation of the huge diocese. Bucer began to preach in Cologne in December 1542; Melanchthon arrived in May 1543. Martin Bucer had become Wied's guiding star in his quest for reform. *The Book of Reformation* composed for Wied by Bucer and Melanchthon appeared in 1543.

Just prior to Melanchthon's arrival, Wied had said Mass in German at Bonn on Easter Sunday 1543 and afterwards distributed Holy Communion under both species. It was a sign of secession, and the pope, Paul III, saw it as such. In a long letter to Wied, the pope expressed his deep sorrow that he should be the first bishop to secede from the Church; he implored him to remember his duty to God, his solemn oath of fealty to the pope. Paul III's pleas were to no avail.

The Catholic resistance to Wied was led by Dr Johann Gropper, the chancellor of the Diocese of Cologne. He was joined by the provincial of the Carmelite Order in Germany, Eberhard Billick, and by the Carthusian Gerhard Kalkbrenner. They formed ranks, and the battle for the faith of Cologne was joined. At this critical juncture, Favre arrived on the scene.

The faithful Catholic leaders in Cologne issued a refutation to *The Book of Reformation*. However they felt that something more than polemics was needed: a strengthening of religion through a revival of devotion and of Catholic practice. Favre's presence in Cologne proved just such a stimulus to popular devotion.

Since the Catholic leaders of Cologne knew Favre at least by repute, they begged him to make representations about the state of affairs in the city to the papal nuncio, Cardinal Giovanni Poggio, and to the imperial court. So, on 27 August, Favre left for Bonn, where the emperor had made a temporary stay. Favre delivered the appeal to Poggio and was able to describe the critical state of the Cologne Catholics to Pedro de Soto, the emperor's confessor, and to the Imperial chancellor, Antoine Perrenot de Granvelle.[61] Favre had already made the acquaintance of Soto and Granvelle from his time in Worms and in Regensburg.

The results of Favre's pleas were at first favourable. Wied, who was present in person in Bonn, promised to dismiss all Lutheran preachers from his diocese, to suppress Bucer's plan of reformation and to make no innovations in the liturgy unless they had been decided by Rome.

Favre's delight at Wied's seeming change of heart was short-lived. The archbishop soon resumed his campaign of reformation as if he had made no promises at all! Nevertheless Favre took up his ministry of giving the Exercises and preaching in the religious houses of the city. On 3 September, he wrote to Cardinal Morone to excuse himself for not having returned straightaway to Mainz. As it happened, he was never to visit that city again. One evening, towards the end of September, a Jesuit student from Louvain, Andrew de Oviedo, arrived in Cologne. He was in a sorry state for, on the way, he had been set upon by robbers and badly beaten. This unfortunate individual had come with a letter from Ignatius ordering Favre to take ship for Lisbon![62]

When news of his impending departure got around, Favre's Cologne friends, more than likely Kalkbrenner and his circle, let Poggio, the nuncio, know that they had some very strong ideas of their own on this matter. They addressed Poggio in a formal petition:

> It seemed to us to be a well-advised move to present a petition to your Reverence ... We ask, indeed with all respect we implore through Jesus Christ, that it be given us to enjoy the singularly delightful presence of the very distinguished theologian, Master Pierre Favre of the So-

> ciety of the Name of Jesus. This we ask that this holy city of Cologne may be kept safe and sound ...[63]
>
> It is of the gravest moment, in view of the thousand heretical snares with which Cologne is beset, that this man ... should remain here to help the sorely tried people with his incomparable wisdom. If necessary, we beg your Lordship to petition the Holy Father, Pope Paul, on our behalf ... [64]

All to no avail! Favre was ordered to leave Cologne for Portugal. Before he left, his Cologne friends presented him with some of their treasures – religious relics! Favre recounts how he left Cologne on 12 July 1543:

> I left the city [Cologne] with seven heads from the holy bodies of the eleven thousand virgins, together with many other sacred relics ... One of these heads had been given to me by the Cologne Charterhouse, another by the convent of St Maximinus ... and a smaller one by the convent of the 'White Ladies'. Two others had been presented to me by the Convent of St Michael. The sixth had come to me from the parish church of St Columba. Alvaro Alfonso gave the seventh into my keeping for Doña Leonora Mascarenhas.[65]

King John III of Portugal had asked for Favre by name. He had heard about him through Diego de Gouveia, by now former rector of Sainte Barbe in Paris. The king wanted Favre to travel with the retinue, which was to escort his daughter, the Infanta Maria, to Spain; she had become engaged to Prince Philip, the future king of Spain. Ignatius judged this an excellent opportunity to ease the way for a Jesuit foundation in Spain.

Favre journeyed to Antwerp in the hope of finding a ship bound for Lisbon. On his arrival in Antwerp, he was told that the next sailing would be after Christmas. He went to Louvain and then fell suddenly ill with a serious fever.

This illness further delayed him by two months. From his sick bed in Louvain, Favre had to restrain the ardour of Peter Canisius and Alvaro Alfonso, who were devoting themselves to works of charity. Apparently they had, perhaps foolishly, put aside their studies in order to labour in hospitals or to wait on poor people whom they had taken under their roof. On his recovery, for his part, Favre took up his usual pastoral activities in Louvain. Favre stayed in the house of one Cornelius Wischaven (1509–1559). Cornelius was already a priest, ministering in the Church of St Peter of Louvain. Toward the end of 1543, Favre accepted him as a Jesuit novice. Cornelius began his novitiate in his own house.

After the feast of the Epiphany, 1544, Favre's previous plans for a voyage to Portugal were cancelled. Instead he sent on a number of young Jesuits, some priests, some still novices, to Portugal. It seems that, for some reason, Ignatius had ordered that the Jesuit scholastics in Louvain be sent to Rome or to Coimbra, Portugal. Such was Favre's attractive character and deep spirituality that he had won over these aspirants to Jesuit life while he was in Louvain.

One of these young men was another Cornelius Wischaven, nephew of the aforementioned. He was only fifteen or sixteen years of age at the time. The day before the young Jesuits were to leave on ship for Portugal, he begged Favre to admit him into the Society and to send him to Portugal with the others. Favre refused on the grounds that this teenager needed to test his vocation under the guidance of his uncle. The young Cornelius, not to be outdone, hid himself on board the ship and, in that way, overcame Favre's resistance! Sadly Cornelius was later drowned in Spain in 1546.

Favre travelled back from Louvain to Cologne in January 1544, bringing with him two young disciples, a Belgian name Lambert Duchateau and Aemilian Loyola, a nephew of Ignatius. Favre rented a house and lived with Peter Canisius and about eight other young Jesuits. This community was supported financially by the local Carthusians and by alms from two noble ladies. Sadly Lambert died of some unspecified illness in late 1544.

In Cologne, Favre preached on all Sundays and important feasts, beginning on the Sunday before Lent and continuing until the end of Easter week. His congregations were made up of university students, priests and canons of the cathedral and others who understood Latin. He heard the confessions of the students and gave spiritual direction. He conducted a retreat at the Charterhouse of St Barbara. Kalkbrenner was among the monks who attended. As a mark of his affection for the monks, Favre gave them a copy of the *Spiritual Exercises* written in his own hand.

All was not easy for Favre's young Jesuit community in Cologne. In gathering his companions under one roof, Favre had unknowingly broken one of the city's laws. Owing to the exemption from municipal taxes that the numerous convents and monasteries enjoyed, the Cologne senate had prohibited the foundation of new religious communities. Archbishop Wied saw his chance and demanded that Favre's community should be dispersed. In addition, Wied's agents in Cologne received instructions to spread defamatory rumours about the Jesuits. If they belonged to a proper religious order why did they not, like other religious, wear a distinctive habit and sing office together in choir?

On 27 July, the senators of Cologne decided to institute an enquiry, and a week later, Favre was officially questioned. He explained exactly who his community was, faithful adherents of the Catholic Church whom the pope had authorised in a special bull to follow the rule of life according to which they were then living. The senators were not convinced and demanded another meeting to discuss the issue. The resolution of the problem would fall to Peter Canisius as Favre would, by this stage, be on his way to Portugal.[66]

In the meantime, Favre's delay in Louvain and Cologne proved an unexpected blessing for the papal nuncio in Germany, John Poggio. Poggio had resolved to use his influence to keep Favre in Germany. By 28 November 1543, Poggio received the authority he sought from Rome to this end. Cardinal Cervini, Poggio's intermediary in Rome, knew nothing of the orders Ignatius had sent to Favre to leave for Portugal. Ignatius, in turn, knew nothing of the negotiations between Poggio and the Holy See! Favre was caught in the middle. As things turned out, Poggio's order prevailed. However, in the spring of 1544, any doubts were resolved for Favre. It seems that the representations of King John III of Portugal prevailed in the Vatican. In May, Favre received word from Ignatius to proceed to Portugal.

On 12 July, Favre left Cologne for the port of Antwerp on his way to Portugal.

## Portugal

Favre's voyage to Lisbon was his first experience of sea travel. Unfortunately we have no account of the voyage. He arrived in Lisbon on 24 August 1544 and travelled on, almost immediately, to the royal court at Évora, some sixty miles east of Lisbon. There he found the Jesuits Simão Rodrigues and Antonio Araoz.[67] Unfortunately Favre was in poor health and low spirits, unable to do much work. He suffered from a bout of depression and a constant anxiety that he was wasting his time at the royal court. While being consoled with news of the missionary achievements in the Far East of his friend Francis Xavier, he felt himself to be doing nothing of value for God or God's people.

In December 1544, Favre went with the King John's leave to Coimbra, where the Jesuit scholastics (students) whom he had sent from Louvain awaited him. All was not well in Coimbra. The community of sixty was in excess of the number permitted by the papal bull;[68] the rector, Simão Rodrigues, had admitted twenty-three Portuguese with little regard for their suitability. They were receiving inadequate training because of Rodrigues's frequent absences at the royal court. During these absences, he left all the scholastics in the charge of one Martin de Santa Cruz, a young priest who was himself a student and a novice! Santa Cruz had a frank interview with Favre about the state of the community and the difficulty of his position – unable as he was to consult his absent superior, Rodrigues. Favre heard the novices' confessions and gave them instructions and exhortations. The students and professors of the university town of Coimbra came to him in crowds for confession and the Exercises.

It is precisely at this time that Favre mentions in his *Memoriale* a 'holy fear' lest the Society of Jesus suffer by reason of the sins committed by present or future members of the same Society. He notes that many enter 'who have in many ways grievously offended God before entering'. Favre resolves to pray especially for 'some of ours' (of the Society) whose general confession he had heard.[69] Clearly there was a need for greater discernment in accepting young men into the Society. Simão Rodrigues had been singularly lacking in his discernment of the suitability of some candidates.

During the month of January 1545, there was very great flooding at Coimbra, destructive in many ways, not only to crops, but also to houses and furniture.[70] Favre prayed that fine weather would come. Although he prays for those who have suffered loss in the floods, his theology leads him to consider such natural calamities as punishment from God for sin.[71] This, to the modern reader, will seem an unattractive aspect of Favre's thought, but we need to bear in mind that Favre was very much a man of his time.

With the Jesuit Antonio Araoz and another companion, Favre left Coimbra around 20 January 1545, and reached Sardoal, south-east of Coimbra, before midnight on 23 January. He wrote at once to the harassed rector of Coimbra, Martin de Santa Cruz:

> We arrived at Sardoal tonight after eleven, each of us with sore feet from causes other than the weather ... Yesterday we could not hire mules so we travelled with one mule between the three of us; each got his third of the mule by day and by night. Blessed be the Lord who is no respecter of persons.[72]

Once again, we see here that touch of humour in Favre, scarce in evidence but still there.

Favre was back in Évora with the royal court by 2 February. He wrote again to Martin Santa Cruz on 3 February, telling him that he had given Simão Rodrigues 'the head of one of the eleven thousand virgins I brought from Cologne'. Favre gives instructions that the history of St Ursula and her companions be read at table in Coimbra for at least three days. This must have been riveting reading! He gave two more of the treasured heads on 24 February to King John and Queen Catalina, the sister of Emperor Charles V. The royal couple had Favre place these gifts in a reliquary in the queen's oratory.

Notes

1. Cardinal Gasparo Contarini (1483–1542), like other cardinals of his time he was a layman. He was an outstanding theologian and was a leader of the reform movement within the Roman Catholic Church. He was responsible for the papal approbation of the Society of Jesus on 27 September 1540.
2. Quoted in Purcell, *The Quiet Companion*, p. 81.
3. See *Spiritual Writings of Pierre Favre*, p. 74.
4. Philip Melanchthon (1497–1560) was a Protestant reformer. He came under the influence of Martin Luther whose teaching he helped to cast into a more rational and systematic form.
5. Quoted in Bangert, *To the Other Towns*, p. 108.
6. Quoted in Purcell, *The Quiet Companion*, p. 80.
7. Martin Bucer (1491–1551) entered the Dominican Order in 1506. In 1521, he secured papal dispensation from his religious vows. He married in 1522. He began to preach Lutheranism in Alsace and was excommunicated by the bishop of Speyer. After the death of Zwingli, he became the leader of the Reformed Churches in Switzerland. In 1549, Bucer came to England and was received with much honour by Edward VI and Thomas Cranmer, and made regius professor of Divinity at Cambridge. He died in Cambridge and was buried there. During the reign of Queen Mary (1553–1558), his corpse was exhumed and burned.
8. Purcell, *The Quiet Companion*, p. 109.
9. John Cochlaeus (1479–1552) was a German humanist and controversialist against the Lutherans. He was present at the Diets of Worms (1521), Speyer (1526 and 1529), Augsburg (1530) and Regensburg (1541).
10. The Diet of Regensburg took place from 27 April to 22 May. The three Catholic theologians were Johann Eck, Julius von Pflug and Johann Gropper; the three Protestants were Philip Melancthon, Martin Bucer and Johann Pistorius.
11. The Lutheran teaching on the Eucharist was as follows: the Body and Blood of Christ are 'truly and substantially present in, with and under the form of consecrated bread and wine (elements) so that communicants eat and drink both the elements and the true Body and Blood of Christ himself'. Lutherans do not hold the same belief as Roman Catholics that the presence of Christ continues in the bread and wine after the time and place of the celebration.
12. Transubstantiation, in the Roman Catholic theology of the Eucharist, the conversion of the whole substance of the bread and wine into the whole substance of the Body and Blood of Christ, only the 'accidents' (i.e. the appearance of bread and wine) remaining. The doctrine of transubstantiation was defined at the Fourth Lateran Council (1215).

13. Robert Wauchope (c. 1500–1551) was a Scots-born cleric. He was a friend of Erasmus. He studied and later taught at the University of Paris. He played a prominent role at the Diets of Worms and Regensburg and, later, at the Council of Trent. He was archbishop of Armagh *in absentia*.
14. Quoted in Bangert, *To the Other Towns*, p. 123.
15. *Memoriale*, 24.
16. Purcell, *The Quiet Companion*, p. 75.
17. Purcell, *The Quiet Companion*, p. 75.
18. Purcell, *The Quiet Companion*, p. 75.
19. *Memoriale*, 22.
20. Quoted in *Spiritual Writings of Pierre Favre*, p. 326.
21. The Spiritual Exercises are divided into four weeks, not of seven days. The First Week is usually of about eight days and prepares the retreatant for an Examination of Conscience and a general confession. The Second Week lasts about eleven to twelve days; the Third, five, and the Fourth, five.
22. Purcell, *The Quiet Companion*, p. 90.
23. Purcell, *The Quiet Companion*, p. 91.
24. Purcell, *The Quiet Companion*, p. 93.
25. *Memoriale*, 24.
26. *Memoriale*, 28.
27. A benefice is a living made from a church office. It can be the property attached to a church office, bestowed on a priest.
28. Cardinal Alessandro Farnese (1520–1589) was the nephew of Pope Paul III.
29. Cardinal Giovanni Morone (1509–1580) was appointed nuncio to Germany by Pope Paul III in 1536 and again 1542.
30. Juan de Aragón was a Portuguese and made the Exercises under Favre. He became a Jesuit, and died in Portugal about 1565. Alvaro Alfonso, a Spaniard, also made the Exercises under Favre. Alfonso attached himself to Favre and began to work with him. On 25 August 1542, Favre sent him on pilgrimage to Trier and to Cologne. Later Alfonso was sent to Louvain to join the community of Jesuit students there.
31. *Memoriale*, 32.
32. Quoted in *Spiritual Writings of Pierre Favre*, p. 334.
33. *Spiritual Writings of Pierre Favre*, p. 333.
34. Otto Truchsess von Waldburg (1514–1573), prince-bishop of Augsburg. Created a cardinal in 1544 by Paul III.
35. *Spiritual Writings of Pierre Favre*, p. 335.
36. The relics of the Three Kings are enshrined in Cologne Cathedral.
37. The Holy Shroud is the Shroud of Turin for centuries purported to be the burial garment of Jesus Christ. Since 1578, it has been kept in the royal chapel on the Cathedral of San Giovanni Battista in Turin.
38. Purcell, *The Quiet Companion*, pp. 115–116.
39. Albert of Brandenburg attained three bishoprics by the payment of ten thousand ducats to the Roman Curia. To recoup himself he engaged Johannes Tetzel, a Dominican friar, to preach on indulgences. Language used by the preacher, for example 'No sooner have the coins jingled in the collection box than the soul is freed from purgatory', led to Luther's Wittenburg theses on indulgences (November 1517).
40. *Memoriale*, 145.
41. Quoted in Brian O'Leary, 'The Discernment of Spirits', p. 95.
42. *Spiritual Writings of Pierre Favre*, p. 189.
43. See *Spiritual Writings of Pierre Favre*, p. 182.
44. *Memoriale*, 233.
45. Esteban Carola was a young man from Speyer whom Favre had taken into his little community and who frequently accompanied him on his journeys – to Aschaffenburg, for instance. He entered the Society and was sent to Rome. His health became so bad in Rome that, in September 1555, he had to be sent back to Speyer to recuperate. He then went to Cologne, where he died on 15 October 1557.
46. *Memoriale*, 209–210.
47. Quoted in Bangert, *To the Other Towns*, p. 165.

48. *Memoriale*, 284
49. Peter Canisius (1521–1597), from Gelderland in Holland, was a Jesuit theologian. He was to compile a number of catechisms of which the chief was *Summa Doctrina Christianae*, published in 1554. He was very active in the Counter-Reformation movement in south Germany. He was canonised in 1925. He is a Doctor of the Church.
50. Dom Gerhard Kalkbrenner was an outstanding benefactor of the early Society of Jesus. He welcomed the Jesuits to Cologne and sent financial support to Ignatius in Rome for the fledgling Roman and Germanic colleges. At the General Chapter of the Carthusians at the Grande Chartreuse in 1544, Kalkbrenner spoke enthusiastically about the newly founded Society of Jesus. Such acclamation induced the General Chapter to seek a spiritual sharing with the Society of Jesus of 'sacrifices, prayers, fasting and other exercises'. See Henry J. Shea, 'Contemplates and Apostles: The Paradoxical Harmony of the Carthusian and Jesuit Charisms', *Studies in the Spirituality of Jesuits*, 55:1 (Spring 2023).
51. Quoted in *Spiritual Writings of Pierre Favre*, pp. 345–346.
52. Quoted in Purcell, *The Quiet Companion*, p.125.
53. Brian O'Leary, 'Discernment of Spirits', p. 26.
54. *Memoriale*, 286.
55. These 'hospitals' were night shelters or refuges for the poor and for wayfarers. They did not provide any treatment for the sick. The early Jesuits often stayed in them overnight or for as few days. Any nonspiritual work they did in them was of the most menial and repugnant kind.
56. *Memoriale*, 286.
57. Quoted in *Mémorial, Bienheureux Pierre Favre*, trans. by Michel de Certeau (Paris: Desclée De Brouwer, 1959).
58. Quoted in Purcell, *The Quiet Companion*, p. 126.
59. Quoted in William Brodrick, *St Peter Canisius* (Chicago: Loyola Press, 1998), p. 44.
60. Quoted in Bangert, *To the Other Towns*, p. 175.
61. Antoine Perrenot de Granvelle (1511–1586) was chancellor of the Holy Roman Empire under Charles V.
62. *Spiritual Writings of Pierre Favre*, pp. 274–275.
63. Quoted in Bangert, *To the Other Towns*, p. 196.
64. Quoted in Brodrick, *Canisius*, p. 50.
65. *Memoriale*, 368. In their Church of St Maximus, the Augustinian nuns had preserved up to 1645 the bodies of the companions of St Ursula. The convent of the 'White Ladies' were also Augustinian religious. They possessed many heads and other relics of St Ursula's companions. The Convent of St Michael was yet another convent of Augustinians. Among their 'treasures' they had the heads of the companions of Ss Gregory and Ursula. As he left Cologne with these grisly objects in his baggage, Favre unwittingly helped to spread one of the greatest frauds ever perpetuated in the history of relics. The not very well authenticated story about a martyrdom in the fourth century, that of St Ursula and a very few companions, grew into one of the most extravagant stories ever told about early Christianity. So when countless human remains, doubtless those of plague victims, were discovered at Cologne in 1255, they were accepted as those of the martyrs. Thus were born the legends of St Ursula and her 11,000 companions. Cf. *Spiritual Writings of Pierre Favre,* p. 278.
66. See Brodrick, *Canisius*, p. 54.
67. Antonio Araoz was a relative of Ignatius by marriage. Born in 1515, Araoz had become a doctor of theology at Salmanca, then went to join Ignatius in Rome. After a period in Naples, he journeyed to Spain with six scholastics who were to study at Coimbra. They reached Coimbra on 8 April 1544. Araoz then went off to the court of John III at Évora, where Favre found him in August 1544. In 1547, Araoz became the first provincial of the Spanish province of the Society, which by then had approximately forty members.
68. This was the Papal Bull of Paul III of 1539 which stated that the Society of Jesus would have no more than 60 members!
69. *Memoriale*, 397.
70. *Memoriale*, 393.
71. *Memoriale* 57, 112, 230.
72. Quoted in Purcell, *The Quiet Companion*, p. 142.

## Chapter 5

# Spain (1545–1546)

The whole idea of Favre's journey to the Iberian Peninsula was that he would proceed from Portugal to Spain. King John of Portugal was reluctant to let him go but eventually, after much vacillation, gave his permission. This reluctance of the king had been very great. Favre, explaining to the Coimbra Jesuits what had happened, used a forceful expression: 'We wrestled, *extorsimus*, from the king what he who sent us [Ignatius] wanted, permission to proceed to Spain.'

On 4 March 1545, Favre and Antonio Araoz left Évora for Valladolid. They arrived in Salamanca on 12 March, merely to stay overnight. We might remember that Favre should have made the journey from Évora to Spain the previous autumn, had illness not delayed his departure from Flanders for several months. He was to have accompanied the Infanta Maria of Portugal to Salamanca and Valladolid for her marriage to Prince Philip of Spain. It was hoped that the Infanta Maria would promote the idea of a Jesuit foundation in Spain. Antonio Araoz was of the opinion that nothing more profitable could be done for the Society of Jesus in Spain than to have its members at the royal court. He described the Spanish court as the *fons universalis regni totius* – 'the absolute source of the universal kingdom [of Spain]'.

Favre and Araoz arrived on 18 March 1545 in Valladolid, where Prince Philip and his Portuguese wife, Maria, had their court. The royal couple, both only eighteen years old, received the two Jesuits hospitably and gave them a lodging next to the Church of Nuestra Señora la Antigua. Favre was very pleased to meet up again with

Cardinal John Poggio, now papal nuncio to Spain, whom he had known in Germany and in the Netherlands.

Mary Purcell tells us that Antonio Araoz, like Dr Pedro Ortiz, had a good opinion of his own preaching powers. In a letter to Rome, Araoz records that on the day he left Portugal 'they paid me the compliment of getting me to give five sermons', and he lists, for Ignatius, all the sermons he gives in Valladolid *and the important people who attended*![1] Favre, as usual, gave his time to the confessional and to personal spiritual direction. Interest in this new religious order (the Jesuits) spread rapidly among the prelates and noblemen of the Spanish court. The omnipresent Dr Pedro Ortiz was also in Valladolid, preaching much about the Society and 'still going strong'.[2] While in Valladolid, Favre and Araoz laid the foundation stone for a Jesuit college. This college would be completed in 1545.

On the eve of the Annunciation (24 March), a sermon was being preached in the royal chapel and Favre went to hear it. The porter, not knowing him, refused him admission. Favre reflects on this experience:

> So I remained there at the door for a while, remembering that I had often allowed various sinful thoughts to enter my soul while leaving Jesus with his Word and his Spirit to knock and stand at the door ... I prayed that it be granted the porter and me not to stand and wait too long before the gates of paradise, undergoing purification ... So it happened that I came to love the porter all the more, he being the cause of my devotion.[3]

Perhaps, because of the new situation in which Favre found himself, his old diffidence and timidity began to revive. Perhaps there is an element of humour in the above extract.

On Good Friday, Favre had to hear the confessions of very small children. A spirit spoke to him inwardly: 'You have not come here to minister to these small children, have you? Would it not be better to be where you could hear the confessions of some important people.'[4]

Favre quickly feels this reaction to be a temptation of the evil spirit and so writes in the *Memoriale*:

> There was revealed to me better than ever the value of these works which, with a good intention, are devoted to little ones and those despised and rejected by the world ... For my part, it was my wish, and I considered it very worthwhile, forever to teach only the unschooled, the children, the countrypeople, the poor and the forsaken.[5]

Around the same time, Favre recalls how he had waited for a young man who had promised to come to confession and had twice disappointed him. Favre was feeling distressed in spirit because he had already wasted, as he thought, six hours on the matter. On further reflection, he is consoled by the Lord with these thoughts:

> If you [Favre himself] are in the habit of spending hour after hour waiting at the doors of great noblemen and princes for the service of God and you do not resent it, knowing that a reward has been stored away for you, why do you feel burdened when some other person, one of Christ's little ones, keeps you waiting? Will God give you less of a reward in this case than in that? How often do you make Jesus stand at your door? And yet you want him not to get discouraged, not to regret having waited; you want him not to be able to feel annoyed, not to be able to become impatient with you or bitter towards you. Be sure then to treat this little one in the same way. Act yourself as you know he would act if his humanity were visibly and locally present in visible flesh.[6]

On yet another occasion, Favre became very sad and dejected to think that he achieved nothing of note. He kept thinking that he could not help being by far the least successful of all his contemporaries (the first companions of Ignatius, the first generation of the Society of Jesus). However the good spirit again consoles him when he reflects that 'the slightest actions done with a blessing of grace are longer lasting and more fruitful than the greatest actions done with little grace'.[7]

During these last few months, Favre was constantly worried about the employment of his time. On 2 March 1545, he wrote to the Jesuit community in Coimbra:

> I earnestly beg you to pray for me to God because I do not know how to make use of precious time, and I am unable to find any time for doing good. Again I ask you, pray to God so that his Divine Majesty may grant me grace not to waste any time but rather to be able and willing to order all the moments of my life according to his holy will.[8]

On 16 April 1545, Favre presented yet another one of the heads of eleven-thousand virgins to Prince Philip! He regrets that he was unable to offer two heads at the same time so that they might be preserved together by the prince and princess, Doña Maria, until one or other of them should die.[9] Sadly such a tragedy was soon to occur.

In May 1545, at the invitation of the cardinal-archbishop of Toledo, Juan Pardo de Tavera, Favre visited the Spanish infantas, Maria and Juana, in Madrid. While at the royal court, he received copies of letters of his old roommate, Francis Xavier. In typical fashion, initially Favre was consoled by the missionary achievements of Xavier, but then he felt himself to be doing nothing for God or for others.

Accompanied by the cardinal, Favre went on to Galapagar, the big market town to the north-east of Madrid, where he had ministered on his previous visit to Spain. They spent some days there, lodging in the presbytery attached to the benefice and the parish that had been made over to Pedro Ortiz in 1542 by Esteban Merino, then nuncio to Paris. Ortiz himself was with them in this presbytery. Cardinal Tavera had Favre read the letters 'from our dearly loved Master Francis Xavier', which pleased the cardinal very much. At Pentecost, Favre returned to Valladolid.

The rejoicing throughout Spain at the birth of a son (Don Carlos) on 4 July to Prince Philip and Princess Maria changed to sorrow when the princess died four days later. The young prince was left a widower at the age of eighteen. Favre wrote a letter of sympathy from Valladolid on 13 July to King John III of Portugal on the death of his daughter. Not having been at the Princess Maria's death bed himself, Favre yet tries to console the king by recounting what he must have heard from others:

> The father provincial of the Dominicans, a person deserving of no less praise than that of a saint, was constantly with her [the princess]. From him and many other persons of like quality further details will be forthcoming on her highness's holy and precious death, and on how well she was prepared for the journey ordained for her by our Lord.[10]

The mourning period for the late Princess Maria over, Prince Philip moved, with the court, to Madrid, having instructed Favre and Araoz to transfer to that city. By then negotiations to establish a Jesuit foundation in Castile were well advanced. Some Flemish and Spanish Jesuits from Coimbra and others whom Favre had received in Spain, with still more sent from Rome by Ignatius, were to form the nucleus of this new foundation.

In the *Memoriale*, Favre recalls a simple but striking episode that occurred on the feast of the Exaltation of the Holy Cross (now called 'The Triumph of the Cross', 14 September). He writes how he was on his way to celebrate Mass when a man approached him asking him to hear his confession. Favre told the man that he would 'willingly be Christ's broom'. He then reflects on how he has various thoughts about this expression, *Christ's broom*:

> Then I came to have various thoughts about that expression. I wished to be put in the same class as the brooms used for sweeping out houses, mainly because I remain wretched and dirty while cleansing others and because I collect all kinds of filth from the improvement which, with Christ's cooperation, I effect in others in my capacity as servant. I saw too how quickly I become worn out like a broom. In spite of this I found much devotion in offering myself to Christ as his household broom for sweeping out spiritual dwellings.[11]

Such a reflection causes Favre to pray that Christ would make use of and shape all future members of the Society into the most menial implements and brooms.[12]

By November 1545, this 'worn-out broom' is arranging for a Jesuit foundation in Alcalà with seven men and sending three other Jesuits to Valladolid.

Favre spent ten days in Toledo in November 1545, giving the Exercises. From Toledo, he wrote to Martín de Santa Cruz in Coimbra. Martín wrote a letter of thanks to Favre, enclosing further copies of letters of Francis Xavier. Favre returned to Madrid on 13 January 1546.

Favre reflects how, during his travels, while staying in inns, he has always felt inspired to do good by instructing and encouraging people.[13] He felt that it was good to leave some trace of good and holy behaviour. In typical fashion, he admonishes himself for often being negligent, above all, in instructing, correcting, admonishing or consoling those whom he had met or merely seen.[14]

Around the end of January 1546, the *Memoriale* breaks off suddenly. In the last entry, Favre writes of experiencing 'a revival of my defects'. He feels the need for 'a new way of recollection of soul'; a need for 'more silence and solitude'. The very human and, therefore, attractive Favre still experiences temptations 'against feelings of poverty [spiritual poverty] and against the temptations of various fears, needs and deficiencies'.[15] And so, the *Memoriale* ends.

Notes

1. Purcell, *The Quiet Companion,* pp. 147–148.
2. Quoted in Bangert, *To the Other Towns*, p. 265.
3. *Memoriale*, 412.
4. *Memoriale*, 421.
5. *Memoriale*, 421–422.
6. *Memoriale*, 429.
7. *Memoriale*, 423.
8. Quoted in *Spiritual Writings of Pierre Favre*, p. 310.
9. *Memoriale*, 430.
10. *Spiritual Writings of Pierre Favre*, p. 377.
11. *Memoriale*, 440.
12. *Memoriale*, 441.
13. *Memoriale*, 433.
14. *Memoriale*, 434.
15. *Memoriale*, 443.

Chapter 6

# The Last Months (1546)

On the Third Sunday of Advent 1545, in the Tyrolese town of Trent, a procession of bishops and priests, chanting the *Veni Creator Spiritus*, proceeded from the Church of the Holy Trinity to the cathedral, where they attended a solemn Mass celebrated by Cardinal Giovanni del Monte. It was the formal opening of the Council of Trent.

No Jesuits were present on the opening day of the Council, but, three days later, Claude Jay arrived as the representative of the cardinal of Augsburg, Otto Truchess. The following February, Pope Paul III asked Ignatius for more of his men for the work at Trent. Ignatius chose Diego Laínez, Alfonso Salmerón and Pierre Favre.

The question of bringing Favre all the way from Spain was not an easy one for Ignatius to decide, and he turned to the other Jesuits in Rome for advice. Before they expressed their opinion, special prayers were said for three days, and each priest offered three Masses, asking God for light to know which would be more to the divine service, Favre's attendance at Trent or the continuance of his work in Spain. With Ignatius voting last and fully aware of the travelling difficulties involved, the decision was unanimous that Favre should bring his Spanish mission to an end. On 17 February 1546, Ignatius wrote to Dr Ortiz and Prince Philip requesting that Favre be allowed to leave Spain.

The order from Rome came as a jolt to Favre. Here was the repetition of what he had gone through so many times before, the abrupt termination of work that was just about under way and so full of promise. In a letter to Simão Rodrigues, Favre tells him that what redeemed this situation was the fact that these changes all originated with orders from his superiors:

> I would not be able to be at peace, except that holy obedience has so disposed. I say this especially in view of the brevity of my sojourns, my departure being ordered at the very time when human reason would have me endeavour to prolong my stay. If it is for me to sow and for another to reap, I would be happy, but there is a lurking fear in my heart that it is my sins that are the cause of these transfers ... I close this letter with the hope that this journey may turn out to be a quest for another Favre, who will have less thought of self and more of you in Christ.[1]

Here again, we see Favre being ever available for mission in virtue of holy obedience to his superiors, and yet, the very human, diffident, self-questioning Favre – qualities which make him an ever more attractive person.

Favre was instructed to visit the Jesuit communities in Valencia and Gandia before he embarked at Barcelona. He left Madrid on 20 April. On Thursday of Easter Week, he arrived at Valencia and, on the following Sunday, reached Gandia where he was to spend a few days with the duke of Gandia, Francis Borgia.

About a month before this Doña Eleanor, Borgia's wife, had died. During their conversations, Borgia asked Favre to carry to Ignatius the news that he, Borgia, had decided to ask admission into the Society of Jesus. The crowning event of Favre's stay in Gandia was on 4 May, when he laid the cornerstone for the college that the duke was erecting for the Society.

Shortly after Favre's departure from Gandia, Francis Borgia made the Spiritual Exercises with the Jesuit Andrew de Oviedo, and, on 2 June, Borgia made a vow to enter the Society.

On 5 May, Favre was back in Valencia where he stayed until 11 May. One person he was especially glad to see was his confessor at

Paris, Juan de Castro, now the prior of the Carthusian monastery of the Valley of Christ.

Favre arrived in Barcelona in the middle of May but a combination of sickness and transportation difficulties held up his departure until early in July.

Favre was suffering again from the tertian ague – a heavy flu. By 12 June, he was well enough to try to find passage across the Mediterranean. One day in early July, he sailed out of Barcelona, and on the 17 July, a little over seven years since he started out with Diego Laínez for the legation in Parma, he arrived back in Rome.

Looking back on Favre's many journeys in only a few years, it is striking that he never had an opportunity to put down roots anywhere. No sooner had his apostolate begun to bear fruit in one place than he was missioned to another: a year in Parma; eight months in Germany followed by five in Spain; back again to the Rhineland where he spent seven months in Speyer; ten in Mainz and almost a year between Cologne and Flanders; finally there was almost half a year in Portugal and fourteen months in Spain. He travelled more than 12,000 miles on foot, on the back of a mule and by sea voyage. And Favre chastised himself for wasting time! His life was an intensely active one; it was also an intensely prayerful one. His apostolate fed his prayer, his prayer nourished his apostolate.

We have no record of the warm welcome that Favre must have received from Ignatius and his Jesuit companions in Rome. His first week in a sweltering hot Rome was spent visiting and being visited. He met with Ignatius on a number of occasions to discuss the situation in Germany. On 23 July, he wrote to Diego Laínez, who was already at the Council of Trent. He sympathised with Laínez over the death of his father and exhorted him to write to his bereaved mother and to other members of Laínez's family. This was the last letter Favre ever wrote. Two days later, on the sixth Sunday after Pentecost, 25 July, he went down again with a fever that worsened daily.

On Saturday, 31 July 1546, Favre received the Last Sacraments. This tireless worker in the Lord's vineyard died peacefully, aged only forty, in the afternoon of 1 August 1546. Ignatius's secretary Fr Juan de Polanco recorded the event:

> Since God in his goodness summoned his Favre to the Council of Heaven instead of the Council of Trent, he was, on the feast of St Peter in Chains, set free from the chains of his earthly life and so took wing for the liberty of heavenly life.[2]

Favre was buried in the little chapel of Our Lady of the Wayside (Santa Maria della Strada) on 2 August. Twenty years later, in 1568, when the Roman Jesuits decided to build the Church of the Gesù over Ignatius's tomb, this little chapel had to be pulled down to make way for the new church. Care was taken to identify and translate the remains of Ignatius; but it was impossible to distinguish Favre's bones from others exhumed at the same time. The remains were all gathered together and reburied under the main door of the Gesù.

When he heard the news of Favre's death, Peter Canisius wrote to Ignatius:

> The death of my father, Master Favre, is not indeed, in itself a matter for tears, but I have to confess that the news was a cruel blow to me. The sorrow in my soul is such that I cannot help expressing a little of it to your Reverence, and I beg you to help my weakness with your prayers.[3]

Among the Jesuits in Rome there were mixed feelings of joy and sorrow. They rejoiced in the assurance that Favre had gone to his eternal reward. Through his secretary Bartholomew Ferron, Ignatius expressed these feelings to Peter Canisius: 'He [Favre] will now help us more than he could have ever done here below. This is the hope and joy that the Lord has poured into our souls.'[4]

Ignatius expresses the same sentiments in a report to the Jesuits in Spain and Portugal:

> After Master Pierre's departure from this sorry world for the next, we herein Rome have been filled with a certain hope. In fact, to be more accurate, I should say that we have been filled with a certain sureness and joy that from his place in heaven, he will help us far more than he has helped us here below in the past, or would be able to do if he had remained among us.[5]

Favre's Jesuit brothers were now convinced that he finally lay at rest from his labours and many journeys.

### The long road to sainthood

In a way, Favre was canonised by universal acclaim at his death, and, since then, no one in his native village of Villaret in Savoy, or in the surrounding district, has ever used his name without the prefix 'blessed' or 'saint'. About fifty years after his death, a chapel, dedicated to Favre, was built on the site of his original home. This chapel housed a wooden statue of Favre, carved locally. Savoyards came to pray there. In 1607, the altar of this chapel was consecrated by Francis de Sales, bishop of Geneva. Francis paid a splendid tribute to Favre's memory in 1608, the year he published his *Introduction to the Devout Life*:

> When the great Pierre Favre, first priest, first preacher and first lector in theology in the holy company of the name of Jesus, and first companion of the Blessed Ignatius, its founder, was on his return journey one day from Germany where he had performed great services for the glory of our Lord and was travelling through this dio-

> cese, the place of his birth, he told one day how he had passed through many heretical places and had gained countless consolations from the guardian angels of the various parishes and, on repeated occasions, had received the most sensible and convincing proofs of their protection ... He related this so earnestly that a gentlewoman, then young, who heard it from his own mouth, repeated it with great feeling four years ago, that is to say, about sixty years after he had told it. Last year, I had the consolation of consecrating an altar on the spot where God was pleased that this holy man would be born, in a little village called Villaret in the midst of our most craggy mountains.[6]

The same St Francis de Sales wrote to a Jesuit, Nicholas Polliens, when he, Francis, was returning a copy of Favre's *Memoriale* that he had borrowed from Polliens:

> It is high time that I return to you the little book [the *Memoriale*] about the holy life of our Blessed Pierre Favre. I refrained from having a copy of it made, because when you sent it to me you referred to it as something reserved to your Society for the present. However I should very much like to have a copy of that account of such a holy life – that of a saint to whom for many reasons I am and ought to be devoted ... I like to think that the Society [of Jesus] will someday decide to honour this first companion of its founder as highly as it has honoured others ... His life ... yields nothing but the sweet honey of devotion.[7]

Very early on, in 1575, as a result of a decree issued by the fourth Jesuit superior general, Everard Mercurian, reading of certain spiritual books by Jesuits, including the *Memoriale*, was discouraged. Jesuit superiors were ordered to keep the manuscript copies of the

*Memoriale* out of general circulation. Controversies about contemplative prayer that troubled the Society of Jesus during the sixteenth century may explain this instruction and reserve about the *Memoriale.*

In 1626, at the request of then superior general of the Society, Mutius Vitelleschi (1563–1645), Jean de Sales, bishop of Geneva and brother of St Francis de Sales, set up an official inquiry into the life of Pierre Favre. This inquiry provided striking evidence of the devotion to Favre that flourished among the Savoyards.

The *Memoriale* led a hidden existence in manuscript form until a Latin text was printed privately in 1853 for use within the Society of Jesus. The first vernacular translation appeared in a French edition published in 1874.

Edmond C. Murphy SJ (1913–1994) made an English translation in the 1980s. Michel de Certeau SJ undertook a critical examination of some sixteen extant manuscripts of the *Memoriale* in preparation for his own French translation.[8]

On each anniversary of Favre's death, and every Christmas, there were processions to Villaret, headed by the local clergy, bearing standards and crucifixes. Votive offerings were left at Favre's shrine, and stories were told of how 'holy Pierre of Villaret' had saved a traveller who invoked him when he fell down a precipice and how the sick and injured who prayed to him were cured.[9]

During Easter Week of 1794, the chapel erected in Favre's honour became one of the casualties of the French Revolution. It was rebuilt between 1823 and 1826.

For 250 years, Pierre Favre remained practically unknown outside Savoy. Then, in the late nineteenth century, a priest, promoter of Favre's cause for sainthood, drew the attention of the Vatican to the fact that a local cult of Favre had existed for centuries and had the approval of the bishop of Annecy. Eventually, on 5 September 1872, Pope Pius IX gave solemn approval for the public devotion to Blessed Pierre Favre. And, finally, on 19 December 2013, Pope Francis signed the document of canonisation.

### Notes

1. Quoted in Bangert, *To the Other Towns*, p. 293.
2. *Fabri Monumenta* (Historica Societatis Jesu, 1972), vol. 48, pp. 839–841.
3. Quoted in Brodrick, *Canisius,* p. 80.
4. Quoted in Bangert, *To the Other Towns,* p. 305.
5. Quoted in Bangert, *To the Other Towns*, p. 306.
6. Francis de Sales, *Introduction to the Devout Life*, p. 107.
7. Letter to Fr Nicholas Polliens SJ.
8. *Bienheureux Pierre Favre, Mémorial.*
9. Purcell, *The Quiet Companion*, p. 179.

# Part Two:
# His Heart

Pierre Favre was an attractive character. He was of a simple nature, perhaps, as Pope Francis said to the journalist Antonio Spadaro, somewhat naïve. He had a natural charm, seemingly at ease with kings and peasants, with cardinals, theologians and even with children. He was gentle, courteous, open to listening patiently to others. He was a very gifted spiritual director and confessor, much sought after by royalty, cardinals, bishops, diplomats, religious and priests. He was totally dedicated to the many missions given to him, spending himself to his utmost. He was almost continually 'on the road' of discipleship. At times, he could be diffident, especially as regards his preaching abilities. His was often a tortured spirit, scrupulous to the extreme. He was super-sensitive to the opinions of others, often cast down if he felt their criticism. He could fall victim to despondency, even depression, when he compared the fruits of his apostolate with those of other Jesuits, feeling that he had accomplished little. In short, Pierre Favre was a very human individual, just like the rest of us.

Quoting from a letter sent to St Ignatius, Pope Francis reminds us of something said about Favre: *It seems that he was born not to stay anywhere.*[1] Favre's incessant travels both within Germany and throughout Portugal, Spain, France and Italy meant that he was often required to find lodgings wherever he could. He recalls with gratitude some of the places in which he stayed but does not hesitate to mention the harsh conditions he so often encountered:

> I was able to recall with feelings of gratitude the many different lodgings in which I had stayed during my lifetime. ... I could not avoid finding myself frequently in places either infected or threatened by all kinds of diseases. I very often spent the nights in filthy hospitals, often again in wretched lodgings, at times in bitter cold and in places destitute of everything except a roof, hay and straw. On occasions I even had to sleep in the open air.[2]

As a life, Favre describes it as 'wandering and restless', but he is consoled in his belief that God intended it to be so, and it was for God's sake alone that he endured such hardships.[3]

Notes

1. Pope Francis, 'Holy Mass on the Liturgical Memorial of the Most Holy Name of Jesus', homily, 3 January 2014, www.vatican.va/content/francesco/en/homilies/2014/documents/papa-francesco_20140103_omelia-santissimo-nome-gesu.html
2. *Memoriale*, 286.
3. *Memoriale*, 286.

## Chapter 7

# Prayerful

Because of his busy and distracting life, Favre felt it necessary to arrange a definite place and time for prayer. At first glance, his devotions seem to have consisted of 'popular' vocal prayer. He tells himself that he should take more care when making the Sign of the Cross each night. Nor should he omit an Our Father, a Hail Mary and the Creed. He will do this after his customary litanies and his Examination of Conscience.[1] Favre was especially fond of reciting litanies. He had a series of what he calls *discursos* – thanksgiving prayers, in the form of litanies. He faithfully recited his Divine Office. He sometimes arose in the middle of the night to pray.

On the way to Regensburg, Favre recalls that he received great consolations in different prayers and contemplations and that he was given many new methods and subjects of prayer as he travelled along. As he drew near to a village or town, he invoked the archangel or guardian angels of that region; he prayed for its inhabitants, especially for those at the point of death. As he passed through mountains, fields and vineyards, he gave thanks to God for the plenty he saw around him. Similarly, he invoked the local saints to take care of these places.[2]

There is a trinitarian dimension to Favre's prayer. He calls Trinity Sunday 'the day of the most excellent and holy Trinity'. He feels that there can be no more worthy object of his faith than the Trinity. He desires that God would be 'all in all' for him – that is that he would contemplate and love God in all things. To be graced with such a gift, he feels that he 'must strive to find Christ, who is the Way, the Truth and the Life'; he must beg power from the Father, wisdom from the Son and goodness from the Holy Spirit.[3] He prays that God the Father will increase his strength, that the right ordering of himself may be guided by the Son and that his desires will be purified by the Holy Spirit.[4]

Among Favre's desires, that for direct union with God is preeminent. These desires have their source in his interior, in his heart (*cor*), ever since St Augustine's day considered the very centre of a person where God comes to fix his abode. Favre pays close attention to these desires and longings in prayer. He studies and scrutinises these motions until they become unambiguous, discovering what is of the good spirit and of the evil spirit. I will treat of this topic later (see pp. 106ff).

## The Mass

Of central importance in Favre's prayer life was the Mass and devotion to the Blessed Sacrament. We need to keep in mind here that Favre's approach to the Mass was, of course, medieval – the priest said the Mass in Latin with his back to the people. It appeared that the Mass was the priest's business, and the congregation assisted, more as spectators.[5] On a personal note, I remember how, as a young altar server, our local parish priest 'got on' with the celebration of the Mass. I would give the necessary responses in Latin, while in the month of October the congregation recited the Rosary aloud. There would be a pause in the recitation of the Rosary at the consecration and then the Rosary would continue. In other months of the year, the people just prayed their personal prayers, while the priest and I carried on with the sacred ritual, behind the altar rails.

Be all that as it may, Favre has some interesting references to the Eucharist in the *Memoriale:*

> On St Bernard's day I found very great devotion at Mass and shed many tears as I reflected on the lessening of honour for the Blessed Sacrament as a consequence of the

> tepid lives of many Christians, and finally by those who leave the Church.[6]

We might remember that the presence of the Blessed Sacrament had disappeared from churches that had gone over to Lutheranism. Among Catholics, Favre noted a growing lack of devotion and respect for the Blessed Sacrament.

There is no lack of devotion to the Blessed Sacrament on Favre's behalf. He writes:

> On my knees, humbly in the presence of the Blessed Sacrament, I experienced great devotion at the thought that Christ was really present there in body and that, as a consequence, the whole Trinity was present there in a wonderful way that is not found in other things and places ... Other things such as images, holy water and churches bring us in a spiritual manner the presence of Christ, of the saints and of spiritual powers, but the Blessed Sacrament brings us in a real manner under these appearances the presence of Christ with all the power of God.[7]

From 1543 on, Favre carried a portable altar on which he celebrated the Eucharist. He had obtained permission for this portable altar from the nuncio John Poggio.

### Struggles and distractions in prayer

While in Speyer, Favre recalls how he began to understand how our Lord had kept him for some days in a state of continual dissatisfaction because he was unable to find devotion in his prayers and meditations, and how the Lord had done so to preserve in him the desire of finding such devotion.[8]

> The more the Lord abandons me to that sadness and to that desire of finding him and the more he causes the

> desire to grow and increase in breadth, in length, and in depth … the greater the favour he confers on me.[9]

Such feelings of sadness, while initially appearing to be a movement of spiritual desolation, are, in fact, a movement of spiritual consolation. Watch where they lead Favre – the 'desire to find devotion'. He 'feels' this desire to be, in fact, a 'favour' from the Lord.

There is a striking, very human moment when Favre berates himself for regulating his clock while reciting the Divine Office. He confesses that there was no need to do so, but he turns this distraction into a petitionary prayer by asking God for the grace of being 'regulated' by him and set in order so as to pray well![10] Again, perhaps, a smile at himself!

Favre looks on desires regarding the apostolate or his own spiritual and moral progress as secondary and as lesser gifts from God. He considers these desires as 'distractions', though they are good, because they hold him back from the fundamental longing which is for God in himself. We have seen too Favre's tendency to compare his apostolic work with the missionary endeavours of other Jesuits, for example, on hearing of the exploits of Francis Xavier in the Far East. This tendency to compare his work with the achievements of others, Favre feels, is not of the good spirit.

While celebrating Mass on 12 August 1542 in Speyer, Favre felt himself somewhat distracted by his desires; one was to edify those present in the congregation, the other to obtain devotion for that very purpose. Thinking over the matter, he experienced grace from the Lord not to consent to feelings such as these, but 'to take care that devotion, which is the immediate knowledge of and feeling for the things of God our Lord … should be desired only for the glory of God and for personal edification'.[11] Such 'selfless devotion' would also be exemplary for the congregation present.

## Prayer and good works

Favre believed that holy desires in prayer lead us, in turn, to the desire to perform good works on behalf of our neighbour. The performance of these good works leads us to good desires. There is a circular movement: prayer – desire – works – prayer – desire – works … Pastoral work nourishes Favre's affective prayer and this, in turn, arouses pastoral zeal in him. He believed that by seeking God in good works, he would more readily find God in prayer than if he sought God first in prayer so as to find God subsequently in good works.

> He who seeks and finds the spirit of Christ in good works makes much more solid progress than the person whose activity is limited to prayer alone … To possess Christ in our actions or to possess him in our prayer often amounts to either an 'effective' or an 'affective' possession … Your life should have something of the Martha and Mary in it … It should unite the active and contemplative lives.[12]

There is no suggestion here of the 'Mary stance' being superior to that of Martha (Lk 10:38–42).[13] We have seen already how Favre spent himself in spiritual and charitable works, in selfless service to those in need. Nevertheless, at times, Favre chastises himself for not using the gifts God has given him in service of his neighbour:

> to crown God's mercies, it has now been given me to see that I am too quiescent in my God and in love for my neighbour and that I am seriously remiss in making use of and in expending so many great talents.[14]

I mention the Martha/Mary image here because this 'mixed life' (prayer/active apostolate), as exemplified by the early Jesuits, was attacked again and again by some cardinals and other religious orders and had to be often and vigorously defended by the Society. We might remember that this new order of 'reformed priests' (the Jesuits) had sought not to have many of the outer trappings of religious life heretofore: choir/office in common, distinctive religious garb, monastic timetable etc. In the words of second-generation Jesuit Jerónimo Nadal, 'The road was their [the Jesuits'] home.' The Jesuit was 'to find God in everything' – Jesuits were not monks!

Because the Jesuit's life was a 'mixed life', Favre fervently believed that the one who seeks and finds the spirit of Christ in good works makes much more solid progress than the person whose activity is limited to prayer alone. In addition, Favre considered that the person engaged in the active apostolate should be gifted with many talents, for without these, they will turn out failures:

> They need a particular kind of patience, humility and charity, accompanied by other virtues for work with the poor and the sick, with sinners, or their persecutors or others… To bring efficacious aid to our fellow men, we need many spiritual lights; we need our eyes, our ears, and our other senses; and, to add to these, we need physical vigour, devotedness, generosity, zeal and other qualities of soul and body.[15]

It is interesting that the qualities that Favre mentioned above mirror his very own attractive, pastoral personality.

## Angels and saints

Pope Francis spoke of the 'somewhat naïve Favre'. This 'attractive' quality of Favre is surely shown in his belief in the protection of guardian angels and the power of intercessory prayer to the saints. Coupled with this belief is his, at times, seeming fascination with the relics of saints.

Like some of the early Fathers of the Church,[16] Favre believed that not only individuals but also nations, towns and cities had guardian angels. Devotion to angels, in general, had entered

Western spirituality through the Latin translations of *The Heavenly Hierarchy* of the Pseudo-Dionysius (late fifth/early sixth century), and in the High Middle Ages through the Cistercian monk Bernard of Clairvaux (1090–1153). This devotion was taken up, in turn, by such mystics as the Belgian Beguine Mechtild of Magdeburg (1207–1282), the German Cistercian Gertrude of Helfta (1256–1302) and by theologians such as the German Dominican Johannes Tauler (1300–1361) and the German Carthusian Ludolph of Saxony (1300–1377). In Spain, the Catalan Franciscan Fra Francesc Eiximenis (d. 1409) wrote a popular treatise on the angels. Somewhat later, the Belgian Denis the Carthusian (d. 1471) made a compendium of practical counsels of the mystics in regard to spirits.[17] It is likely that Favre would have come across some of these writings through his contacts with the Carthusians in his youth and, later, in Paris and Cologne.

Devotion to guardian angels had spread widely in Europe during the fifteenth and sixteenth centuries. Favre had a special devotion to guardian angels.

On entry into a city, town or even house, Favre would invoke the guardian angel of that place. These 'good angels' or 'good spirits', he believed, would protect him and all those with whom he came in contact. Favre would greet people while invoking the protection of their guardian angels on their behalf. He believed that something very necessary for retaining a person's goodwill was to have a great devotion to his/her guardian angel, 'for they can predispose people toward us in many ways and curb the violence and temptations of our enemies'.[18]

Depending on where he was, Favre had great devotion to the local saints. In Germany, he venerated the Magi (whose relics were said to be in Cologne Cathedral); the 11,000 virgins, especially St Ursula and St Pinosa ('whose head and the very arrow I saw with my own eyes in a certain Benedictine monastery'). In France, he had devotion to St Genevieve, to St Denis the Areopagite, to Mary Magdalene. In Savoy, he mentions his devotion to St Bruno, the founder of the Carthusians, and, interestingly, to Pierre Veillard, his old tutor, whom he considered to be a saint. He writes of saints who may have died in Europe, Africa or Asia, thus revealing his belief in the communion of saints.[19]

Favre sees this devotion to the saints as being 'in conformity with the true faith', which teaches that it is a holy thing to invoke the saints, particularly for certain graces for the spirit or the body. Favre's target here is the Lutherans, who criticised devotion to the saints as a superstition. The Lutherans believed that such devotion limited God's power and the efficacy of God's action.[20]

One example of Favre's simple devotion might suffice. While in Mainz, Favre recalls his early devotion to St Apollonia of Alexandria (+249), virgin and martyr, whose execution had begun by having all of her teeth violently pulled out or shattered. Favre tells us that, as a child, he was accustomed to read a prayer to this most holy virgin, a practice he had begun because of a toothache he had. He never suffered from toothache afterwards, and so he thanked this saint who had so readily obtained for him the preservation of his teeth![21]

## Sacred objects

Favre was deeply attached to relics of all kinds and profoundly affected by crucifixes, statues, the decoration in churches and chapels, ceremonies with incense, music and chanting. We need to remember that the cult of the saints and relic hunting were all part of 'religious' practice in the sixteenth century.

For Favre, sacraments, sacred images, sacred music, relics and processions all served to stir up religious feelings; above all to strengthen faith, hope and love. Sacred objects were, for him, signs of what they represent; they make their way into the soul and there awaken these three virtues. Favre believed that the use and contemplation of these objects was especially suited to 'lowly and simple folk'. In the *Memoriale*, he writes that in the cathedral in Mainz he was aware of a clear understanding about the usefulness of images of the saints: 'in order to make them present to us anew'. So he begged God to make Christ present in his mind 'through the vivid representational power possessed by the images of saints in the eyes of the devoutly believing Catholic faithful'.[22]

Favre's 'naivety' in relation to sacred objects is seen in an episode he recalled while saying Mass in the church called the Church of the Holy Cross, outside the city of Mainz.

> In that church there are some objects that keep alive the memory of those celebrated miracles that took place there in former times. One of these objects, a crucifix, was found floating on the Rhine and moving upstream against the current; another crucifix – still kept there – after having its head knocked off by a blow from some mocker, began to bleed. To this day the blood can clearly be seen to have flowed down the statue.[23]

However, Favre does not always receive spiritual consolation from these sacred objects or relics. He recalls that while saying Mass in a chapel of the archbishop of Mainz, which, for Favre's sake, had been splendidly adorned with all the archbishop's relics and treasures, Favre found himself in a state of total spiritual aridity. He feels that this felt state was a grace from Christ crucified, who 'deprived him completely of any longing he had to seek in these "outward shows" a means either of increasing interior devotion or of finding Christ crucified with more success'.[24] Perhaps Favre had detected illusion somewhere in this brilliant display.

On 24 May 1543, while in Mainz, Favre recounts how during a Corpus Christi procession he was moved to devotion at the sight of a variety of things used to embellish the procession, how in this ritual all the human senses had a part to play, how all parts of a human body could find something useful to do. There was a place for singing and for the playing of instruments. Country folk brought along branches, greenery and woven wreaths, and craftsmen too added their efforts in different ways. 'So, it happens that all men in all ways, even physically, have a means of serving Christ and submitting their whole bodies to him from whom they have received them.'[25]

In the vivid description of this procession, Favre may have had a polemical purpose: the justification of external rites in worship against the Lutherans who maintained a purely spiritual or interior worship. Acts of public and external worship, such as Corpus Christi processions, were criticised by Lutherans. Favre, for his part, held that the more these external testimonies were despised and treated with indifference, the more they were needed.[26] He was saddened at the thought that Germany might one day lose all these testimonial aids to devotion, the heritage bestowed by centuries of loving artistry and craftsmanship.

Earlier, while in Speyer in 1541, Favre recalls how

> at first vespers of the Assumption, I found great spiritual devotion when I was in the Cathedral of Our Lady of Speyer. This was because the ceremonies, the lights, the organ, the chanting, the splendour of the relics and the decorations – all these gave me a great feeling of devotion that I could not explain it. I blessed the person who had placed the votive lights there, lit them and arranged them in order for that purpose. Likewise I blessed the organ, the organist, the benefactors, and others as well as all the priestly vestments ... So too, the choir and the sacred music sung by the boy choristers, and I blessed in the same way the reliquaries and those who had sought out relics and adorned them fittingly when found.[27]

Again we need to bear in mind that the Lutherans would look somewhat askance at some of the features mentioned in the above quotation.

### Care of the sick

Care of the sick was one of the constant ministries of the first Jesuits. It was a crying need everywhere at the time, a true corporal work of mercy, since there were no hospitals in the modern sense of the word – 'hostels' might have been a more appropriate word for such institutions. This pastoral care needed a strong stomach. Care of the sick in one of these 'hostels' was one of the 'experiences' or tests imposed on Jesuit novices. To this day, it is usual for a Jesuit novice to spend some time serving in menial work in a hospital or hospice or, at least, among the poor and needy.

Favre recalls that

> having arisen in the quiet of the night to pray, I felt strongly inspired to do my utmost to provide for the needy and the homeless sick wandering about the city of Mainz, a hospice where they could be gathered together and given shelter so as to receive treatment there and recover their health.[28]

Again, Favre berates himself for 'the many acts of negligence and forgetfulness and my want of concern for a number of beggars whom he had seen not so long ago, covered with sores'. He recalls how he had helped these poor sometimes but in an offhand and reluctant manner. For although he was without resources, he now writes that he could have seen to it that others came to their aid. He himself could have begged from door to door some additional relief for the poor and indigent.[29]

Neither pestilence nor the perils of war had any power to hinder the movement of Favre's charity. In all the cities he visited, he could be found wherever human misery dragged out its course. Whether Catholic, Protestant or Jew, it made no difference; for their troubles were the only necessary passport to his heart.[30]

**Notes**

1. *Memoriale*, 58.
2. *Memoriale*, 21.
3. *Memoriale*, 307.
4. *Memoriale*, 317.
5. *Spiritual Writings of Pierre Favre*, p. 124, footnote 192.
6. *Memoriale*, 92.

7. *Memoriale*, 352.
8. *Memoriale*, 63.
9. *Memoriale*, 64.
10. *Memoriale*, 249.
11. *Memoriale*, 81.
12. *Memoriale*, 125.
13. The idea that the contemplative life was superior to the active life goes back as far as Origen (c. 185–254). See James Harpur, *Dazzling Darkness: The Lives and Afterlives of the Christian Mystics* (London: Hurst, 2025), p. 20.
14. *Memoriale*, 353.
15. *Memoriale*, 127.
16. Reference in Matthew 18:10. St Jerome (347–430) stated that sin drives guardian angels away. Honorius of Autun (1080–1151) held that every soul is assigned a guardian angel the moment it was put into the body. Thomas Aquinas (+1274) wrote that guardian angels were the lowest order of angels. A feast of guardian angels was founded in Portugal in 1513, and was extended to the whole Roman Catholic Church by Pope Clement X in 1670 (2 October).
17. See O'Leary, 'Discernment of Spirits', p. 72.
18. *Memoriale*, 34.
19. *Memoriale*, 28.
20. See *Spiritual Writings of Pierre Favre*, p. 176, footnote 83.
21. *Memoriale*, 244.
22. *Memoriale*, 350.
23. *Memoriale*, 308.
24. *Memoriale*, 209.
25. *Memoriale*, 322.
26. *Memoriale*, 215.
27. *Memoriale*, 87.
28. *Memoriale*, 159.
29. *Memoriale*, 159.
30. See Brodrick, *Canisius*, p. 33.

Chapter 8

# Compassionate

The rapid success of the Lutheran and Calvinist preachers in Germany was attributable, in no small measure, to their use of the vernacular and their ability to translate, with eloquence and verve, the language of scholars and theologians into the everyday speech of the people. Remember that Martin Luther had translated the New Testament into German, as spoken by the people. He had composed hymns that would instill Lutheran beliefs into their minds and hearts. Luther would later translate the whole Bible into German so that it would be accessible to all.

Ignorance of the German language seriously impeded the apostolate of almost all the early Jesuits. Favre was no exception. He never learned German; he used Latin, understood and spoken only by educated people, or Spanish, because it was the language of the imperial court. Favre's hearers in Germany, then, were a select, educated audience.

Arising from his own personal experience in Worms and Regensburg, Favre had little faith in diets and colloquies. He was convinced that such gatherings between Catholics and Lutherans only gave the Lutherans splendid opportunities for spreading their doctrines by sermon and pamphlet, in the vernacular and in racy language intelligible to all.

In his correspondence and his letters, Favre often refers to the Lutherans as 'heretics'. In our more 'ecumenical' age, such language and thinking would certainly not be appropriate or helpful! In general, Favre looked upon Lutherans as lapsed Catholics to be won back to the faith; he had no understanding of the convinced

Lutheran or of the strength of that Lutheran's theological position. Nevertheless Favre did not hate the Lutherans and deplored any attempt to coerce them back into the Church by force of arms; above all, he prayed for their leaders.

Favre has a very striking entry in his *Memoriale* for 9 November 1541:

> On the day of St Elizabeth, queen of Hungary, I felt great fervour as eight persons became present to me along with the desire to remember them vividly in order to pray for them without taking notice of their faults. They were the sovereign pontiff, the emperor, the king of France, the king of England, Luther, the Grand Turk, Martin Bucer and Philip Melanchthon. That came about through experiencing how severely these men were judged by many; as a result, I felt for them a certain kind of holy compassion accompanied by a good spirit.[1]

Later on, in 1546, in the final months of his life, while in Coimbra, Portugal, Favre recalls how 'I was affected by a feeling of deep compassion for all those who are in manifest danger of damnation. Luther, the king of England, the Grand Turk, and some others came to mind.'[2]

Furthermore, Favre asked God to have mercy on the German nation and 'to have compassion on it as if it were already suffering all those evils which are in store for it, if not drawn back to the Catholic faith and allegiance to the religion of Rome'.[3] He genuinely believed that these Reformers were on the road to eternal perdition! Remember that the teaching of the Catholic Church at that time was that outside the Roman Catholic Church there was no salvation.[4]

Favre had written on 28 May 1543 to his cousin, the Carthusian Claude Perissin, prior of Le Reposoir: 'I am beginning to realise that these heresies of our time are nothing else but a lack of devotion, humility, patience, chastity and charity.'

For Favre, the process of abandoning the Church begins with tepidity, which gives rise subsequently to intellectual aberrations. For him, faith is not a cold intellectual assent; it 'is always God's gift moulded by love' (*fides caritate formata*).[5]

Favre always held that moral and affective causes lay at the root of the Reformation. The German people had lost their way morally. By 1544, he was fully convinced that moral reform preceded rather than followed the recovery of the Roman Catholic faith, and that reform began with the clergy rather than with the people and with the individual rather than the community; and so, as we have seen, much of Favre's apostolic activity was directed toward the Catholic clergy, maybe especially toward those who were vacillating in their faith. He believed that true reform begins gently and gradually from within the Church and under the influence of the Holy Spirit, from whom it will derive its efficacy.[6] In stark contrast, he considered that God does not approve of the way in which 'heretics' wish to reform certain things in the Church. He is willing to concede that though the 'heretics' say (as do the demons) many things that are true, they do not say them with the spirit of truth which is the Holy Spirit.[7]

A letter written by Peter Canisius to Ignatius in 1544 reports that Favre and the reformer Martin Bucer met in disputations in Bonn several times. Canisius relates how Favre was 'able to prove to Bucer and other heretics the truth of the faith he himself professed'. There is no mention of such meetings with Martin Bucer in the *Memoriale*; but, since the focus of the spiritual diary is on Favre's interior experience, such an omission does not preclude these meetings having taken place.[8]

The second-generation Jesuit Pedro de Ribadeneira writes of Favre 'forcefully holding back the fury of the heretics, repeatedly engaging their leaders and teachers, especially Bucer, so fiercely and bravely'.[9] This description of Favre's method of direct dialogue with the Reformers is so much at odds with what we have already seen of Favre's gentle, pastoral approach, as to be judged a total fabrication.

It would appear that Favre's contacts with Protestantism were, for the most part, indirect; aside, perhaps, from the debates with Bucer and some Protestant leaders in Bonn. His dealings were with Catholics who had already left the Church or were contemplating that step. He could not but regard such Catholics as lost or straying sheep to be brought back to the fold, to the teaching and authority of the Catholic Church. He reveals no real understanding of the strength of Protestant convictions.

In stark contrast to Ribadeneira's portrayal, in a letter to his brother Jesuit Diego Laínez, written from Spain and dated 7 March 1546, Favre counsels Laínez on how to deal with 'heretics' (Lutherans). He advises a friendly, compassionate and loving approach to them; they being people who need spiritual help. Favre stresses the importance of personal relations and points of agreement with the Lutherans over theological argument. One should avoid any debate in which one side tries to put down the other.[10]

It is fascinating to read, in this letter, how Favre advises Laínez to speak to the Lutherans about what will lead them to good works. Remember that Martin Luther was teaching that the Christian is justified before God by faith alone and not by good works. Favre suggests that Laínez speak to the Lutherans simply about 'how to live well'.

A further quotation from this same letter to Laínez reveals so much about the delicate, sensitive, gentle pastoral approach that Favre adopted:

> Anyone wanting to help the heretics of this age must be careful to have great charity for them and to love them in truth, banishing from his soul all considerations which would tend to chill his esteem for them. The next thing he must do is to win their good-will and love by friendly intercourse and converse on matters about which there is no difference between us, taking care to avoid all controversial subjects that lead to bickering and mutual recrimination. The things that unite us ought to be the

> first ground of our approach, not the things that keep us apart.[11]

Though, while counselling such a gentle approach, Favre himself was often deeply depressed about the state of religion in the Rhineland. In a letter to Ignatius from Mainz, dated 7 November 1542, Favre writes that 'God knows what I went through in Speyer, struggling against despair of any good for Germany.'[12]

The spiritual renewal of the German nation within the fold of the Catholic Church was at the heart of Favre's apostolic concern. But the difficulty of the task, his personal shortcomings and what he saw as the desperate state of the Church in Germany sometimes threw him into such despair that he was tempted to leave the country altogether:

> I pondered on that torment which has never left my mind since I first came to know Germany: the dread of its total defection from the faith … that thought … strives particularly to bring me to outright despair of bearing any fruit, first by leading me to contemplate flight and then by provoking in me the desire to leave the Rhineland and so abandon the position entrusted to me there. Oh, would that there were an immediate end to that instability of mine that has so often brought me to imagine at one time that everything looked successful and flourishing and, at another, that a situation was desperate or that all had been lost.[13]

Favre identifies this feeling with his natural spirit of diffidence. This 'bad spirit' must be driven out or, at least, ignored. He realises that this will not be easy, given his faults and his tendency to be excessively influenced by the opinions of others.[14]

We have seen that Favre had a natural diffidence as regards preaching, preferring to let others, such as Laínez or Ortiz, engage in this ministry of the Word, while Favre would reap the fruit of such preaching in confessions or in spiritual conversation. While in Speyer, however, after finishing Mass on 3 September, he was greatly moved in spirit by a desire to preach. He writes, 'I then resolved more firmly than before to make every effort so as to be able to preach or lecture in Germany, for otherwise a serious trouble would be born of so much prolonged silence.'[15]

Later, in Mainz, in December 1542, by command of the cardinal of Mainz, Favre was giving a course of lectures on the Scriptures. He noted that he was becoming somewhat clearer and was, to some degree, getting rid of that incoherence and confusion that was natural to him. He felt that his memory too and his powers of retention were improving.[16] Favre attributes this to the effect of a mystical grace he had received. Before that he lacked coherence, his memory was faulty and he suffered from nervousness.[17]

Notes

1. *Memoriale*, 25.
2. *Memoriale*, 390.
3. *Memoriale*, 44.
4. This opinion was first taught by Cyprian of Carthage (+258). However, Cyprian was referring to babies who had been previously baptised by heretics. The teaching was also held by the Fourth Lateran Council (1215) and by the Council of Florence (1441). Thankfully it is not the teaching of the Roman Catholic Church today. Such an unhelpful teaching may explain why Favre's friend and roommate St Francis Xavier was in such a hurry to baptise thousands of babies and adults in the Far East with minimal or no prior Christian instruction.
5. *Memoriale*, 218.
6. *Spiritual Writings of Pierre Favre*, p. 97.
7. *Memoriale*, 51.
8. Mention is made of this meeting with Bucer in *Spiritual Writings of Pierre Favre*, p. 35.
9. Ribadeneira, *The Life of Ignatius of Loyola*, p. 255.
10. *Spiritual Writings of Pierre Favre*, p. 379.
11. Quoted in Brodrick, *Canisius*, p. 35.
12. *Spiritual Writings of Pierre Favre*, p. 339.
13. *Memoriale*, 329.
14. *Spiritual Writings of Pierre Favre*, pp. 256–257, footnote 229. See also O'Leary, 'Discernment of Spirits', pp. 23, 49, 102.
15. *Memoriale*, 112.
16. *Memoriale*, 192.
17. *Spiritual Writings of Pierre Favre*, p.182, footnote 106.

Chapter 9

# Sensitive

Favre analysed his moods with regard to his apostolate in Germany. These moods went from optimism to pessimism and back again. He discovered that the 'good spirit' of optimism was to be welcomed because it was apostolically fruitful, but the 'bad spirit' of pessimism should be banished because it was apostolically sterile.

Favre records how while, in Mainz, on Easter Monday, 1542, he fell back again

> onto my long-familiar cross, that depression with its triple cause: first, my not being conscious of any signs of God's love for me in proportion to my desires; second, my feeling within me, more than I would wish, traces of the old Adam; third my inability to bring forth all the fruit I desire for the salvation of my neighbour.[1]

There is so much contained within this entry: Favre's not feeling spiritual consolation from the Lord, a spiritual consolation he so much desired; the 'old Adam' may be those temptations to sexual impurity that had plagued Favre all his life; and, then, the feeling of not being apostolically fruitful.

Favre has a tendency to be very hard on himself. He is strikingly honest. This, surely, is where the attractive, very human, sometimes fragile Favre comes to the fore. From reading the *Memoriale*, one can only marvel at Favre's total generosity to all, his constant availability for mission, his endless travel, the attractiveness of character of this man. Nevertheless he berates himself for his apostolic 'sluggishness' when there was no need, and he admits to himself and to the Lord his natural physical temptations against chastity:

> My spirit was entirely drawn away from those things which, as it recognised a long time ago, were the places of peace; and my flesh was totally immersed in those things in which, ever since childhood, it had discovered death for itself and disquiet. Disorder in my actions, sluggishness and want of spiritual perception seemed to have come again to life ... With justice was I afflicted; with justice did I walk in sadness, downcast in the midst of that turmoil that sorely tried my spirit, my soul and my body.[2]

Favre mentions a 'triple disorder' in an entry for 4/5 February 1543:

> It [this depression] is almost always made up of three parts: the first concerns my inmost self, when I observe in my flesh such great inconstancy in the pursuit of sanctity; the second lies all about me ... when I see all the works of charity towards my neighbour that I leave undone; the third concerns what is above me, when I recognise my lack of devotion and my remoteness from what has directly to do with God and his saints. The consideration of these three torments of mine from a human standpoint has long since laid upon my shoulders a cross with three arms, the weight of which frequently overwhelms me.[3]

On 29 November 1542, while in Mainz, Favre writes of 'a heightened consciousness of what I might call the cringing and despondent state of my spirit'.[4] He must have been unusually depressed to have used the word *reptilitas* (the quality of creeping and cringing like a snake) in a description of his interior state. But his prayer here was for the grace to devote himself to growth in hope and to raise himself up in spirit. He begged for an elevation of his mind through God's grace so that instead of being habitually stooped and drawn downward in its abjection towards that 'spirit which causes its infirmity', his mind might, through the grace of Christ, devote itself rather to growing in that life that consists in 'looking ever upwards'.[5] In typical Ignatian fashion, Favre begs for the grace necessary to 'act against' (*agere contra*) the temptations from the evil spirit that would render his apostolic work sterile.

**Notes**

1. *Memoriale*, 277.
2. *Memoriale*, 268.
3. *Memoriale*, 241.
4. *Memoriale*, 184.
5. *Memoriale*, 184.

## Chapter 10

# Discerning

Spiritual discernment means to separate things, to discriminate, to notice what is happening both inside and outside myself. Spiritual discernment helps us to put order on our tangled loves and desires; it is about choosing what is life-giving for myself, for others, for our world.

By 'spirits', St Ignatius meant affective stirrings within us: feelings of joy, hope, enthusiasm, generosity, compassion, love, forgiveness; or their opposites: sadness, despair, indifference, cynicism, anxiety, anger, bitterness, self-protection. It is helpful to remember that these affective stirrings are pre-moral; they sometimes just seem to visit us, unbeckoned. We don't choose to feel something. What matters is what we do with the feelings that visit us. Where does the feeling, the affective stirring lead us?

We have seen how Favre's moods vacillated between optimism and pessimism, causing him to change his mind about the likelihood of bearing fruit in Germany. While in Mainz in 1543, Favre notes how he reflected on the different kind of spirits that often agitated him, causing him to change his mind about the likelihood of bearing fruit in Germany:

> I often became aware that in no single instance should we give assent to the words of that spirit who insinuates that everything is impossible and keeps on bringing up difficulties. We should rather attend to the words and the effects of the spirit who suggests possibilities and inspires courage. We must make use discernment so that … we

> may avoid mingling our hopes with illusions that feed on abundance or adding to our fears through a discouragement induced by penury.[1]

The evil spirit causes Favre sometimes to doubt his natural gifts, to think that he is capable of nothing, that he knows nothing and has no hope of helping others. The good spirit, in contrast, leads him along a path entirely the opposite. This good spirit shows him countless things that appear easy of execution, giving him confidence and much courage for those undertakings which surpass the powers of many. In that way, Favre is roused up to continue his service in the Lord's vineyard, instead of giving way to discouragement. The evil spirit is not only evil but a liar as well.[2] We see in Favre's reflections here echoes of the Rules for Discernment of Spirits in the *Spiritual Exercises* of St Ignatius.[3]

On 27 December 1542, Favre offered Mass, praying to overcome a certain coldness in his manner that he was then feeling. He acknowledges that the source of this relational coldness is the evil spirit, which frequently turns him so much against his neighbour and his neighbour against him that they find each other intolerable and can not engage in mutual correction. Favre writes of 'diabolical influences' at work here:

> I mean those influences that cause men to close their hearts to each other and habitually prevent one from tolerating the other in such a way that, if there is something that needs correction, they do not know how to set about it or have no will to do so, preferring rather to sever relations completely because of the trouble stirred by that spirit of division.[4]

This temptation 'to sever relations' is so contrary to what we now know of Favre's character, his consistent courtesy and his openness to others.

The good spirit always brings Favre spiritual consolation; the evil spirit spiritual desolation.[5] Brian O'Leary helpfully points out the priority to be given to the affective element over the intellectual element as being one of the cornerstones of Favre's theory of discernment.[6]

Notes

1. *Memoriale*, 254.
2. *Memoriale*, 156.
3. Rule Two: 'It is the way of the evil spirit to bite, sadden and put obstacles, disquieting with false reasons, that one may not go on; and it is proper to the good to give courage and strength … easing, and putting away all obstacles, that one may go on in well doing.'
4. *Memoriale*, 199.
5. Rule Three: 'spiritual consolation is every increase of faith hope and charity … which calls and attracts to heavenly things … quietening one's soul and giving it peace'. Rule Four: 'spiritual desolation … moves to want of confidence, without hope, without love, when on finds oneself lazy, tepid, sad and, as if, separated from one's creator and Lord'.
6. O'Leary, 'Discernment of Spirits', p. 112.

## Chapter 11

# Gentle

We have seen how much time and energy Favre devoted to the hearing of confessions no matter where he was, however briefly. He considered this to be a crucial ministry. There is a fascinating letter[1] written by Favre in late January 1544 to the Jesuit Cornelius Wischaven[2] in which he gives some pastoral instructions on how Wischaven should hear confessions. These instructions tell us much about the mild, gentle, attractive and compassionate character of Favre:

> When hearing confessions, be mild and gentle. Never permit yourself to speak sharply or show repugnance, no matter how uncouth the penitent. Let us take care not to become bored with this sublime and sacred task, we who represent Christ taking away the sins of the world. Let us take care that no sinner who comes to confession … faces an ordeal when he approaches us, the vicars of the gentle Christ. Let us beware of acting the haughty, disdainful Pharisee, or the angry, impatient judge … Let us do our utmost to ensure that every penitent leaving the confession will freely return there.[3]

In the same letter, Favre writes more specifically on how Wischaven should treat a penitent's individual sins and on how to exhort the penitent to prayer. In questioning penitents about their sins, Favre exhorts Wischaven, the confessor, to choose his words carefully. He should try to get the penitents to look into themselves and state their sins without fear or any intimidation stemming from his (Wischaven's) words or manner. Sensitivity towards the penitent is of the essence.

To the modern reader, the 'penances' Favre recommends to be given to the penitent might appear a little demanding:

> As a penance you could give them something to memorise ... prescribing that they learn the Ten Commandments or the articles of faith [the Creed] by such and such a day. Or you could direct them to visit churches to obtain indulgences, or hospitals and prisons to practise the works of mercy ... A given penitent might be told to furnish some poor person with clothes.

Favre admits that 'sometimes it is necessary to be hard', but the confessor should make sure that his parting with the penitent is on good terms, except in cases where a person absolutely refuses to give up his sins. Such people may never be given absolution, for example, 'persons who live in concubinage, practise usury or refuse to pay the debts they are capable of paying'.[4] Where a sin involves satisfaction or retribution, it should be immediately dealt with and resolved. Favre recommends St Gregory's *Pastoral Care*[5] as a helpful guidebook to the confessor in this specific matter.

Favre obviously sees the time of confession as an opportunity for catechesis. The penitent should be given specific instructions on prayer: what prayer is, when one should pray and how. The penitent should know the various litanies invoking God and the saints. We have seen how fond Favre was of litanies in his own prayer. Wischaven should teach the penitent the mysteries of the life and passion of Jesus Christ. This was a popular devotion of the time. We might remember that it is highly unlikely that many penitents would have access to a personal copy of the Gospels. The penitent should be taught the elements of the catechism: the Ten Commandments, the precepts of the Church,[6] the seven deadly sins.[7] There should be definite guidelines for almsgiving. One wonders how a confessor would manage to cover even one of these instructions during a time of confession! Perhaps Favre has a more long-drawn out confession in mind, more in line with spiritual direction.

Favre concludes this long letter with the words 'Charity is patient, is kind, it believes all things, hopes all things, suffers all things, endures all things. Charity never fails.'[8] Favre was the patient, kind confessor in whom princes, cardinals, bishops, nobles, ordinary folk and even children found a welcoming and gentle listener.

Notes

1. *Spiritual Writings of Pierre Favre,* pp. 356–361.
2. Cornelius Wischaven (1509–1559) was the first Flemish Jesuit, greatly influenced by Favre. He was eventually called to Rome by Ignatius in 1547. He became novice master in Rome and in Messina, Sicily.
3. Quoted in Purcell, *The Quiet Companion*, p. 68.
4. *Spiritual Writings of Pierre Favre,* pp. 356–361.
5. A treatise on responsibilities of the clergy written by Pope Gregory the Great (+604) around the year 590 AD.
6. See *Catechism of the Catholic Church,* 2041–2043.
7. Seven deadly sins: pride, greed, anger, envy, lust, gluttony, sloth.
8. 1 Corinthians 13.

## Chapter 12

# Obedient

It will, hopefully, be clear that Favre was an obedient Jesuit. We have seen that he was always ready to obey the wishes of those whom he considered to be his superiors at the time – primarily the pope, Ignatius, kings and cardinals.

He was ready to go where, he trusted, he was being sent by these superiors. He was, perhaps, somewhat diffident in this regard – often waiting for an explicit command from his superiors and not trusting enough in his own judgement.

Favre wrote to the young Jesuits in Coimbra in December 1544, telling them that their obedience to their Jesuit superiors must be 'blind': that is, the truly obedient Jesuit must not wait to be assured of the reason for or the sense of the fruitfulness of the work commanded him, rather Favre exhorts the scholastics to remember that a Jesuit, in obedience, 'must never settle down to rest in any place or in any particular work subject to obedience, even if he experiences a holy and unmistakable spirit for it – nor rest in it, I mean in such a way that he loses his readiness for whatever obedience may enjoin'.[1] Favre, himself, was immediately available for mission. He lived what he enjoined on others in this regard.

There is a self-abnegation in the vow of obedience. For Favre, the Jesuit must deny himself, his own wishes, his own views, will and judgement. He must instead submit himself entirely to the wishes, views, power, will and judgement of his superiors.

If the religious superior appears less good in his position, the more perfect will the subject make himself in his own position, which is that of an obedient, diligent and faithful servant in the fear and the love of God our Lord.[2]

Favre recalls how the Lord delivered him from different spiritual motions and moods of despondency by virtue of a holy and blind obedience that did not take into account his personal insufficiency or the magnitude and gravity of what has been imposed on him.[3]

We have already seen Favre's devotion to the Trinity. Favre addresses some prayers to the Trinity when pondering on obedience.[4] He asks the Father to make Favre his 'son' in obedience; the Son to make him 'servant'; the Holy Spirit to make him a 'disciple'. So Favre sees obedience as being essentially to the Triune God. The words he uses – 'son', 'servant', 'disciple' – express different aspects of obedience, and this obedience, Favre holds, can be achieved at every moment and in every action.

The phrases 'blind obedience' and 'submission of wishes, views, power, will and judgement to one's superior' will appear off-putting to the modern reader. Perhaps it will be a consolation to be assured that this is not the way Jesuit obedience 'works' today. The Jesuit superior listens prayerfully and attentively to the desires and inclinations of the Jesuit, and the Jesuit, in turn, will listen to the desires and needs of a Jesuit province (region), told to him by the Jesuit provincial. Together both the provincial and the Jesuit will listen to the prompting of the Holy Spirit and discern what is best for the individual and for the mission. This, at least, is the ideal Jesuit way of proceeding!

**Notes**

1. *Spiritual Writings of Pierre Favre*, p. 371.
2. *Memoriale*, 39.
3. *Memoriale*, 145.
4. *Memoriale*, 40, 41.

# Epilogue

In a homily delivered at the Church of the Gesù, Rome on 3 January 2014, Pope Francis spoke of Favre as being a modest, sensitive man with a profound inner life. He reminded the Jesuits gathered there that Favre was a restless, unsettled spirit who was never satisfied; he was a man of great aspirations; he was aware of his desires. Favre, according to Pope Francis, had a deep and true desire 'to be expanded in God'. He was completely centered in God and, because of this, could go in a spirit of obedience throughout Europe, dialoguing with everyone with charm while proclaiming the Gospel. Favre's familiarity with God led him to understand that interior experience, in prayer and discernment, and apostolic life always go together. He wrote in the *Memoriale* that the heart's first movement should be that of 'desiring what is essential and primordial, that is, the first place be left to the perfect intention of finding our Lord God'.[1]

'Dialogue', 'discernment', 'frontiers' – these are the words that came to Pope Francis's mind when he pondered the life and apostolic career of Pierre Favre. It will now be obvious, I hope, how appropriate these words were in describing Favre's life and ministry.

Pierre Favre, in his own prayer and in his tireless ministry, allowed himself to be touched deeply in his heart by Jesus Christ. Favre, in turn, touched the hearts of many, offering them the gentle approach of selfless spiritual and human friendship, while bringing spiritual consolation to their minds and hearts.

Pierre Favre believed that all ministry should be by way of the heart – God's heart touching his own heart, and so, through him, touching the hearts of his neighbours, whoever they may have been.

One of the first companions, Simão Rodrigues, paid Favre this tribute in 1579, many years after Favre's death:

> In his dealings with others, he [Favre] revealed such a rare and delightful sweetness and charm as I have never to this day, I must admit, found in anyone else. In some way or other, he used to make friends with people, and by the kindness of his manner and speech so won his way into all hearts that he set them on fire with the love of God.[2]

Surely, this is a fitting tribute to this much-loved and well-deserved saint! He was 'so gentle and loving'[3].

Notes

1. *Memoriale*, 63.
2. Quoted in *Spiritual Writings of Pierre Favre*, p. 32.
3. Spadaro, 'A Big Heart Open to God', *America*.

# Prayers and Spiritual Counsels of Pierre Favre

You may like to ponder and pray upon these personal prayers and counsels of St Pierre Favre. The numbers in brackets refer to the paragraphs in the *Memoriale.* The italics are mine.

*May it please God our Lord to grant me the grace* of increasing each day so as to become a *larger vessel,* one of greater capacity and interior cleanliness, made ready to deny entrance to the bad spirits and to admit the good ones. (88)

There is no more effective way to overcome harshness, anger and whatever is contrary to charity than if you are so *meek* that you do not return blow for blow but, welcoming everyone with *kindness,* leave your attacker free to do what he pleases. At long last, otherwise never, his heart will yield and soften at the sight of your *patience* and the depth of your *goodness.* (121)

*Holy desires in prayer* are ways of disposing us to perform good works and good works lead us to holy desires. He who seeks and finds the spirit of Christ in good works makes much more solid progress than the person whose activity is limited to prayer alone ... Your life should have something of the *Martha and Mary* in it ... it should unite the active and contemplative lives. (125)

Grow therefore, O my soul, in devoted *veneration of all the holy and blessed objects* that have been marked by the Sign of the Cross.

Each day exercise yourself more and more in contemplation of them. (133)

With great fervour and a total new awareness, I wished and prayed that I might at last be allowed to become *the servant and minister of Christ who consoles*, helps, delivers, heals, liberates, saves, enriches and strengthens. I asked that I also, through him, might be enabled to come to the aid of many, to console and free them from many ills, to deliver and strengthen them, to bring them light not in spiritual matters alone but also (if I may be allowed the boldness of presuming it in God) in a material way, together with whatever charity can do for the soul and body of any of my neighbours. (151)

*Seek grace for the smallest things,* and you will also find grace to accomplish, to believe in and to hope for the greatest things. Attend to the smallest things, examine them, think about putting them into effect, and the Lord will grant you greater. Extend yourself and give yourself up fully to doing what you can with a little grace from God and the Lord will grant you a great grace that will enable you to perform even what is beyond your capabilities. (153)

If you have but a *single talent's worth of knowledge and faith,* trade with it and make it yield two (Mt 25:14–30). Take care not to bury it in the ground, and do not say that you need two talents' worth of knowledge before you will set to work ... You must, by trading and working with that one talent, gain another one, and so forth. Do not neglect those everyday duties of yours and those that lie ready at hand, to engage instead in idle contemplation of future undertakings and of others finished long ago. (154)

*Many dream of almost impossible undertakings* and, in the meantime, do not give any thought to the work they have in hand. (154)

*You frequently judge*, looking only to yourself, and to outward appearances, that you are capable of nothing, that you know nothing and have no hope of helping others. But the Lord, in his Spirit, is leading you along a path entirely the opposite. He shows you countless things that with him appear easy of execution; he gives you confidence and much courage for many undertakings which surpass the powers of all people. In that way you are roused up to labour instead of giving way to discouragement about everything. (156)

*May the infinitely good and great God* direct, set right, order and purify all things according to the gracious purpose of his will and make me seek not only who he is in himself but also what he wants of me. (161)

It is often an advantage to us not to experience great devotion in our prayer. We must learn *to labour* on with little grace ... to co-operate with the little grace from God so as to make the best of what is in us and depends on our efforts. We should prize highly not devotion alone but also the *longing quest* for it and even sorrow at our not possessing any of it. (173)

*O my Lord, I beg you to take from me whatever divides*, separates and distances me from you and you from me. Take from me whatever dries me up, makes me inflexible, sends me astray and enfeebles me. Take from me all that makes me unworthy of your visitation ... of your consoling words ... of your kindness and love. (187)

*Have mercy on me, O Lord,* have mercy on me always; drive far from me all that hinders me from beholding you; from hearing you and delighting in you; from touching ... and ever remembering you; from understanding you and hoping in you; from possessing and loving you; from abiding in your presence and beginning to find delight in you. (187)

*It is in the Spirit* that we ought to live out the remainder of our lives and to work in all things for the service of our neighbour and for the praise of God. In the past we have lived enough – overmuch – for ourselves and for our conduct as if we had been born for ourselves alone. (194)

I offered Mass [prayed] ... against a certain coldness in my manner [its source being the evil spirits] which frequently turns me so much against some [people] and them against me that we find each other intolerable and cannot engage in mutual correction. (199)

*When we first begin to lead a better life,* it is as a rule, and rightly so, our principal concern to make ourselves pleasing to God by preparing for him in our bodies and in our spirits a spiritual and corporeal dwelling. *But there comes a time ... when we are inspired – and are indeed bidden – to seek and to tend not so much to be loved by God but to love him.* This means that we should seek him not so much as he is in us but rather as he is in himself and in other created things, and we should seek to know what greatly pleases and displeases him in his creatures. *The first attitude of mind, then, is to draw God to us; the second, however, is to draw ourselves to God.* (203)

*Do not seek the root of the tree* for the sake of the fruit, but rather the fruit and the other things for the sake of the root ... Seek to tarry ever longer as days go by and to strike deeper roots where this tree has its roots, but do not seek to have its fruit remain in you. By its roots and not by its fruit will you be led to the glory of this tree. (280)

*Be in no way disturbed* even if the old Adam in you grows up again stronger than ever ... Be not troubled if you find no fruit at all from your external labours in your hands nor do others who observe you closely so as to imitate you or to delight in the good that you are doing, or those again who watch in order to calumniate you or those who look on your with contempt. (279)

*He who does not have consolation in himself* or does not find any source of consolation is quickly overwhelmed by the burden of the critic. On the other hand, he who has or thinks he has a source of consolation in himself will speedily recover from criticism. It follows that you should be cautious when reprimanding those who are exceedingly dissatisfied with themselves, for they will be overly discouraged unless they are admonished tactfully. (419)

Favre wrote to the Jesuits in Coimbra: *Live happily in Christ and serve the Lord with joy.* (2 March 1545)

# Select Bibliography


Abbott, Walter M., *The Documents of Vatican II* (Geoffrey Chapman, 1966).

Bangert, William V., *To the Other Towns: A Life of Blessed Pierre Favre, First Companion of St Ignatius* (Ignatius Press, 1958).

Bertrand, Dominique, *Pierre Favre un Portrait* (Lessius, 2007).

Brodrick, James, *The Origin of the Jesuits* (Longmans, 1940).

— *The Progress of the Jesuits (1556–1579)* (Longmans, 1946).

— *St Ignatius Loyola: The Pilgrim Years* (Farrar, Straus and Cudahy, 1956).

— *St Peter Canisius* (Sheed and Ward, 1935).

Carberry, Patrick, ed. *With Christ in Service: Jesuit Lives through the Ages* (Messenger Publications, 2017).

*Catechism of the Catholic Church* (Veritas, 1994).

Certeau, Michel de, *Mémorial: Bienheureux Pierre Favre* (Desclée de Brouwer, 1959).

Clancy, Thomas H., *An Introduction to Jesuit Life* (The Institute of Jesuit Sources, 1976).

Conwell, Joseph F, *Impelling Spirit: Revisiting a Founding Experience: 1539 Ignatius of Loyola and His Companions* (Loyola Press, 1997).

— *Walking in the Spirit: A Reflection on Jerónimo Nadal's Phrase 'Contemplative Likewise in Action'* (The Institute of Jesuit Sources, 2003).

— *A Brief and Exact Account: The Recollections of Simão Rodrigues on the Origin and Progress of the Society of Jesus* (The Institute of Jesuit Sources, 2004).

Dalmases, Cándido de, *Francis Borgia: Grandee of Spain, Jesuit, Saint* (The Institute of Jesuit Sources, 1991).

Fleming, David L., *The Spiritual Exercises of Saint Ignatius: A Literal Translation and A Contemporary Reading* (The Institute of Jesuit Sources, 1978).

Futrell, John Carroll, *Making an Apostolic Community of Love: The Role of the Superior according to St Ignatius of Loyola* (The Institute of Jesuit Sources, 1970).

Goulding, Gill K., *A Church of Passion and Hope: The Formation of an Ecclesial Disposition from Ignatius Loyola to Pope Francis and the New Evangelization* (Bloomsbury T&T Clark, 2016).

Guibert, Joseph de, *The Jesuits: Their Spiritual Doctrine and Practice: A Historical* Study, trans. William J. Young (The Institute of Jesuit Sources, 1964).

Lacouture, Jean, *The Jesuits: A Multibiography* (Counterpoint, 1995).

Lécrivain, Philippe, *Paris in the Time of Ignatius of Loyola (1528–1535)*, trans. by Ralph C. Renner (The Institute of Jesuit Sources, 2011).

Leitner, Severin, 'The Spirituality of Peter Faber', in *Review of Ignatian Spirituality,* 109:36 (2005).

Mitchell, David, *The Jesuits – A History* (MacDonald, 1980).

Murphy, Edmond; Padberg, John W.; Palmer, Martin E., *The Spiritual Writings of Pierre Favre* (The Institute of Jesuit Sources, 1996).

Nadal, Jerónimo, 'From the Sixth Exhortation', in 'Spiritual Conversation', in *The Way* (July 2023), pp. 27–29.

O'Leary, Brian, 'The Discernment of Spirits in the *Memoriale* of Blessed Pierre Favre', in *The Way Supplement*, 35 (1979).

— *To Love and to Serve*: *Exploring the Ignatian Tradition: Selected Essays* (Messenger Publications, 2020).

O'Malley, John W., *The First Jesuits* (Harvard University Press, 1993).

Osuna, Javier, *Friends in the Lord*, trans. by Nicholas King (The Way Series, 1974).

Palmer, Martin E.; Padberg John W.; Mc Carthy, John L., *Ignatius of Loyola: Letters and Instructions* (The Institute of Jesuit Sources, 2006).

Purcell, Mary, *The Quiet Companion* (Gill & Macmillan, 1970).
Ravier, André, *St Ignatius Loyola and the Founding of the Society of Jesus*, trans. by Maura Daly (Ignatius Press, 1987).
— *Le Grand Pierre Favre, 1505–1546* (Éditions jésuites, 2017).
Ribadeneira, Pedro de, *The Life of Ignatius of Loyola* (The Institute of Jesuit Sources, 2014).
Shea, Henry J. 'Contemplatives and Apostles: The Paradoxical Harmony of the Carthusian and Jesuit Charisms', in *Studies in the Spirituality of Jesuits*, 55:1 (Spring 2003).
Spadoro, Antonio, *Pietro Favre: Servatore della Consolazione* (La Civiltà Cattolica, 2013).
Sweeney, Jon M., *Peter Faber: A Saint for Turbulent Times* (Loyola Press, 2021).
Worchester, Thomas, ed., *The Cambridge Companion to the Jesuits* (Cambridge University Press, 2008).
Young, William, *Finding God in All Things: Essays in Ignatian Spirituality* (The Library of Living Catholic Thought, 1958).